GOSP

Other Titles in the Biblical Classics Library:

GOSPEL
AND
WISDOM

Israel's Wisdom Literature
in the Christian Life

GRAEME GOLDSWORTHY

PATERNOSTER
PRESS
CARLISLE, UNITED KINGDOM

First published 1987

This edition 1995

01 00 99 98 97 96 95   7 6 5 4 3 2 1

Paternoster Press, P.O. Box 300, Carlisle CA3 0QS, U.K.

British Library Cataloguing in Publication Data

Goldsworthy, Graeme
  Gospel and Wisdom:Israel's Wisdom
  Literature in the Christian Life. – New
  ed – (Biblical Classics Library)
  I. Title II. Series
  223.06

  ISBN 0-85364-651-1

Typeset by Photoprint, Torquay, Devon
and printed in the U.K. by Cox and Wyman Ltd., Reading

FOR MIRIAM,
AND ALSO KAREN, STEPHEN,
DAVID & MICHELLE

Contents

Preface

At the layman's level it is still popular to classify the books of the Old Testament under the headings of Law, History, Prophecy and Poetry. This is a curious arrangement and not a little misleading. The law books are full of history, the history books contain much prophecy, the prophecy books are largely poetry, and the so-called poetry books are so diverse that their poetic content is one of the least useful marks of description. Moreover, there are large slabs of prose to be found in them. It is a matter of real concern that the category of poetry books obscures one of the important areas of literature found within it: the wisdom books. Wisdom is a significant concept in both the Old and New Testaments. It is a key dimension of the Christian life, and finds its centre in the person of Christ. Those books which tell us most about the wisdom of the Hebrews should not be confined to the limbo of a box labelled Poetry.

There are some very readable books available today which investigate the subject of Old Testament wisdom literature. A number of these are acknowledged in my footnotes. However, it must be said that there is a singular dearth of such books which go on to raise the question of the relationship of Old Testament wisdom to the New Testament in general, to Christ in particular, and to the Christian life. My aim in this book is to apply the method of biblical theology in order to place the wisdom literature in its Christian context, that is, to try to understand it as Christian Scripture.

Since it is also my aim to present this material with as few technicalities as possible, the discussion may at times appear to the theologically trained reader to be simplistic or even patronizing in style. I hope this will not be taken as denoting an imprecise analysis of the evidence. To the reader who is not theologically trained I would say that some technicalities are inevitable in any kind of serious study. The reader's lack of familiarity with certain ideas should not be taken as a sign that the material is difficult in itself. A little patience and perseverance is all that is needed in such cases.

I have restricted footnotes to the minimum necessary to fulfil my obligations to clarify concepts, to acknowledge my sources and to make it possible for anyone to verify my references. Where such references are to works of a specialized and technical nature, I have attempted to incorporate the insights of these and other studies into a simple and basic discussion. Overall, I have endeavoured to keep in mind the practical value of wisdom for the Christian life, to remove it from the domain of an élite group, and to return it to its rightful place among all the people of God.

I wish to acknowledge my indebtedness to my teachers at Union Theological Seminary, Richmond, Virginia: Professor John Bright and Professor Patrick D. Miller Jr. who supervised my doctoral studies in the wisdom literature of the Old Testament.

GRAEME GOLDSWORTHY
St. Stephen's Anglican Church,
Coorparoo, Queensland

1

The House on the Rock

Summary

Practical questions such as guidance and decision making are closely related to what the Bible teaches about wisdom. Our starting point is Jesus Christ because he links us through his gospel to God and thus to reality. Wisdom is concerned with the nature of reality. The four Gospels portray Jesus as the wise man above all others. In so doing they build upon the Old Testament's teaching about the nature and place of wisdom in the lives of God's people.

Decisions! Decisions! Decisions!

We all have those days when we are faced with a seemingly endless stream of situations demanding decisions. They can be exhausting times, especially when the decisions are important ones that will affect the course of our lives. We cannot escape decision making. It is a part of being human. Because we are concerned about the results of our decisions, we want to make the right ones. But all too often we find ourselves saying, 'If only I had done this and not that.' The 'if only' disease is a crippling one because it destroys our confidence in future decisions. It breeds an indecision which stifles our ability not only to face life, but also to go out and enjoy it. Indecision is an aspect of our sinfulness because it expresses a problem not only in our knowledge or under-

standing of the world, but in our whole relationship to the
world and to God. It is not surprising, then, that the Bible
says a great deal about decisions and how we make them.

The four Gospels depict Jesus as one who by his very
presence demanded a decision from people. In his teaching
the summons was to faith and commitment, not merely to
receive interesting information. As then, so now; the response
that we make to his entry into our world has results for eternity. Consider the conclusion to his Sermon on the Mount:

> Therefore everyone who hears these words of mine and puts
> them into practice is like a wise man who built his house on
> the rock. The rain came down, the streams rose, and the
> winds blew and beat against that house; yet it did not fall,
> because it had its foundation on the rock. But everyone who
> hears these words of mine and does not put them into
> practice is like a foolish man who built his house on sand.
> The rain came down, the streams rose, and the winds blew
> and beat against that house, and it fell with a great crash.
>
> (Matthew 7:24–27)

The message of this vivid word picture is clear. Those who
take notice of what Jesus says build their lives on a firm
foundation, and those who do not heed it have chosen a
foundation of shifting sand for their lives. It is not
comforting to be compared to a house crashing into a
swirling flood under the buffeting of the wind and the rain.

The point is that Jesus' words demand decision and no one
can remain neutral before them. According to the New
Testament, life's decisions can be made in a way that leads
to either life or destruction. This is the thrust of the
evangelist's challenge to 'decide for Christ', that is, to
believe the gospel. Before Christ, no decision is a 'No!'
decision. The decision we make about Jesus Christ will
affect every other decision that we will subsequently make.
And here lies the difficulty, for it is here that we start to ask
questions about the will of God for our lives. The house on
the rock must, in a sense, be built up from the foundations.
But how do we discern the plan, and what if we should make
a wrong decision? Some decisions are easy in theory because
there is clear scriptural teaching about them. Certain ethical

questions and matters of Christian behaviour involve the uncomplicated application of Scripture. Of course, there are also complicated moral questions which we find more difficult, but it helps to know where to search for an answer.

There is another area of decision-making in life which is not nearly so clear-cut. Every day you and I make up our minds on all kinds of matters, some of which are important to us, others of which are trifling. Many have no obvious relationship to moral principles derived from the Bible, and are not clearly connected with questions of godliness or righteousness. A decision one way or the other would seem in no way to involve us in immorality or in a compromise of the gospel. What we have for dinner tomorrow is largely a neutral decision, provided that the overall pattern of our diet is one of reasonable care for our bodies. But what career we choose, what church we decide to join, what prospective spouse we choose, are all matters of great importance. Some options are already ruled out by Scripture. We do not choose an immoral career, an apostate church, or an unbelieving spouse. But that may still leave us with a number of live options in each case.

One of the things we link with wisdom is the ability to make the right decision. James tell us that if we lack wisdom we should ask God and wisdom will be given to us (James 1:5). So, we ask, and we expect that God will in some way guide us and prevent us from making the kind of decisions that will backfire on us. James reminds us that we should ask God in faith. What exactly does that mean for the way we go about our decision-making? From time to time I have spoken to Christians who are convinced that the gift of wisdom means nothing less than God handing down to believers ready-cut solutions to all their problems. On first sight that may be an attractive prospect. No more worries! No more weighing up all the *pros* and *cons*. No more agonizing over the possible outcomes of our choice of action. All we need do is wait on God for his leading to the right decision. The question is, of course, does God promise any such thing? Is wisdom really a hot-line to heaven, and is God in the business of steering our lives like that? Unfortunately when Christians come to this way of thinking they often become impatient of careful study of the Bible. Their decisions are not made consciously on the basis of what the Scriptures say and the principles they contain, but rather on the basis of some vague and subjective feeling about the Lord's will in the matter. The Bible does say a great deal about guidance and decision-making, but I suspect that some popular notions about these important matters are not really based on the scriptural evidence.

The beginning of wisdom

This book is not primarily about guidance but about the biblical idea of wisdom. The relationship between wisdom and guidance will, I trust, become very clear from the evidence we are to examine. When I wrote *Gospel and Kingdom*[1] to provide a Christian understanding of the Old Testament, there was one quite deliberate omission because of the need to be brief. Questions of Israel's piety (especially as found in the Psalms) and of her quest for knowledge and understanding (as found in the wisdom literature) were not dealt with. It may therefore have seemed to the observant readers of that work that I had conveniently ignored an important area of the Old Testament which did not fit neatly into the proposed scheme of the revelation of the kingdom of God. I intend to show in this book that such was not the case. I hope to demonstrate that, despite the difficulties, the wisdom literature of Israel can be related to her covenant faith, and that it, along with the prophetic promises, points to the coming of Christ.

So my first concern is to look at the whole question of how a Christian may read and apply to himself as Christian Scripture the books of Proverbs, Job and Ecclesiastes, and other parts of the Old Testament that we classify as wisdom literature. Over the last fifty years or so there has been a tremendous renewal of interest in Old Testament wisdom on the part of biblical scholars. Unfortunately not a lot has been done to translate the results of this scholarship into the language of the ordinary Christian untrained in the technical

1. Exeter: Paternoster Press, 1981.

side of biblical studies. This book is intended as a contribution
in that direction.

The word *wisdom* suggests a concern for the way we
think, the way we use our minds or intellects. If that is what
wisdom in the Bible is all about then we have established an
important point: God gave us minds and he expects us to use
them. We have only to look at the way that the New
Testament speaks of the mind to be convinced of this. Paul,
for example, links the renewal of the mind with the
transformed life of the Christian (Romans 12:2). He reminds
us that conversion includes the conversion of the mind. The
Greek word for repentance (*metanoia*) literally means a
change of mind. Furthermore, when the Bible speaks of the
heart it refers to the whole willing and thinking side of our
being. It is what goes on in the head. The fruit of the gospel
in our lives includes the conforming of our minds more and
more to the mind of Christ. This process of becoming holy,
or sanctification, is worked by the Holy Spirit dwelling
within the believer. The Spirit works in and through us.
Thus we are consciously involved in the struggle to become
more Christ-like and to do good works.

If you are one of those people who had a well-defined
conversion experience when you became a Christian, you
will easily recognize that your conversion included a turn-
about in the way you thought about reality. You would not
have worked out many of the implications of this at the
beginning. But at least you will have recognized that God is
somehow involved in all aspects of your experience in a way
that you never recognized as an unbeliever. From this point
on you can never look at reality in exactly the same way you
did before your conversion. The process has begun of
conforming both thinking and doing to the will and character
of Christ. Thinking and doing can never be separated.

When we speak of a sanctified mind, many Christians will
think exclusively of a morally pure mind. Conversely, a
sinful mind will be thought of in terms of moral impurity.
We need to broaden our understanding beyond the moral
dimensions. To think Christianly with a sanctified mind is to
think of reality in terms of the truth that is revealed in
Christ. A sinful mind-set is one which views reality apart

from what God has revealed. It may think high and noble
thoughts of humanitarian kindness, but to the extent that the
truth of God is left out of reckoning that mind-set is sinful.

The Christian mind-set comes about through the gospel,
and so we must come to think of Christian wisdom as a
conforming of the mind to the gospel. If, then, we understand the gospel only in its basic terms of Jesus dying for us,
we will probably wonder how this can affect the way we
think totally. We need to remind ourselves that the simple
gospel is also profound. The truth, 'Jesus died for me',
actually implies everything that God has revealed in the
Bible about his relationship to humanity and to the created
order. Growing as a Christian really means learning to apply
the fact of the gospel to every aspect of our thinking and
doing.

I have indicated two basic areas in which the Bible deals
with the subject of wisdom. They are the wisdom books of
the Old Testament and certain parts of the New Testament.
Specifically it is Jesus Christ who is God's wisdom and who
reveals it to us. The fact that the Old Testament points to
Christ suggests that the wisdom which centres on the gospel
is related to the wisdom which exercised the authors of the
Old Testament wisdom books. The biblical concern for
wisdom should be the concern of every Christian and not
merely of those we might class as intellectuals. A primary
purpose of Israel's wisdom was 'for giving prudence to the
simple, knowledge and discretion to the young' (Proverbs
1:4). There is never any suggestion in the Bible that wisdom
means having an above average I.Q. In the Old Testament
wisdom is not the property of some élite class, as it seems to
have been in some other ancient peoples. In the New
Testament it is asserted that wisdom belongs to all who
believe the gospel.

In the Book of Proverbs the wise man is seen urging his
pupils in the task of acquiring wisdom or understanding of
life. 'Get wisdom', he says (Proverbs 4:7), but what is it and
how do we get it? It seems to wear many faces, yet behind
them all, even the worldly ones, we sense a common factor
which is hard to pin down. To one person wisdom is a
property owner making a shrewd investment, or a statesman

whose political activity seems to pay off for the community in renewed prosperity. To another it is the successful handling of the tricky business of the generation gap in families, or the cool and effective management of a sudden crisis. To yet another it is a monk or a mystic meditating on life and its meaning. Perhaps we can begin to understand wisdom as the reflective thinking which places human beings above the animals. As Christians we will need to approach all definitions with caution and be prepared to adjust them in the light of the Bible. In the Bible the range of wisdom is no less perplexing. In one place it is a proverb about an ant, in another it is a sublime poem about the Creator and his creation. It is a way of thinking and a way of doing. It is a way of teaching and a way of expressing ideas in writing. On the one hand it is to know man and the world, and on the other it is both the way to know God and the reward for knowing him. Then, in the New Testament, there is a worldy wisdom which is really foolishness, and there is God's true wisdom revealed in Jesus Christ.

Since Jesus Christ is the fulfiller of the Old Testament, he alone can bring us to an understanding of the full meaning of the Old Testament wisdom books. On the other hand, the New Testament presupposes what the Old Testament teaches, in order to present the message of Christ. Since the two Testaments depend upon each other, it may appear difficult to decide where to begin. But upon reflection we see that we must begin with Christ because it is through him that we become Christians and are motivated to study the Old Testament as Christian Scripture. We really have two tasks when we approach the Old Testament. First, we want to see how the Old Testament increases our grasp of the New Testament message about Christ. Secondly, we apply our knowledge of Christ as the fulfiller in order to understand the real significance of the Old Testament. When we start with Christ in the gospel and go back from there into the Old Testament, we find that the Old Testament eventually leads us back again to Christ. He is, after all, the author and perfecter of our faith (Hebrews 12:2), he is the Alpha and the Omega, the First and the Last (Revelation 22:13).

When Jesus concluded the Sermon on the Mount with the

illustration of the wise and the foolish builders, he spoke with an authority that the sage and the scribe never had; he spoke as the source of all true wisdom. Nothing Jesus ever said or did would support the idea that the gift of wisdom means that God makes our decisions for us. What he did say was that receiving his words and doing them is wisdom. The person and work of Jesus provide us with the only reliable basis for understanding ourselves, our experience and the world. Within that framework of understanding we must seek to make our decisions as responsible human beings. In our concern to build aright the house of our life, we should remember that the foundation rock is the word of Christ. It is not a mysterious thing that is revealed to us in some secret experience of our hearts. It is there for us in the Bible. We may be tempted to think at times that our decisions have resulted in a rather strange looking house being built on the rock. But Jesus' words should reassure us. If it is built on the right foundation the house will endure.

Questions for study

1. What kinds of problems do Christians have in making decisions and knowing God's will?
2. In what way does coming to know God through Jesus Christ alter our understanding of ourselves and of the world?
3. What does Genesis 1:26–28 tell us about relationships between God, mankind and the created order?

2

Christ Our Wisdom

Summary

All problems concern relationships of some kind. Our relationship to God is perhaps the greatest of all problems. The answer to this, and to all other problems, lies in Jesus who is the perfectly wise man in his relationship to God. Jesus' teaching about wisdom and his constant use of wisdom sayings prepare the way for Paul's statements about Christ as our wisdom. Wisdom is a characteristic of the person who is rightly related to God. Jesus came to be the truly God-related man for us, and therefore he is wisdom for us. One outworking of this in our lives is that our way of thinking about all things is changed through the gospel. True wisdom is a result of being related to God through the person and work of Christ.

Identifying the problem

The Christian life is lived in an enormously complex world. In some ways the complexity is increased by our Christian faith because we find ourselves at loggerheads with the mindset of the unbelieving world. Those who long for the relative simplicity of the 'good old days' would have to admit that they probably did not have fewer problems in the past, only different ones. Our lives are made up of discoveries, decisions and relationships which give to us a sense of the meaningfulness of our existence. People who have no sense of being related to other people or to the world find life without meaning. The problem we all face is that of knowing what is in life and knowing how to get it all together. Failure to achieve any kind of integrated view of reality can lead to severe mental illness and even death.

There has never been a lack of preachers ready to tell us that Christ is the answer. But it has been well remarked: 'If Christ is the answer, what is the question?' This reminds us of the need to be precise in how we think of Christ as the answer to our problems. It is the gospel which shows us both the problem and the answer. In doing this it speaks mainly in terms of relationships. For example, the biblical definition of man is primarily a statement of how he relates to God, to himself and others, and to the world. The whole creation and fall narrative in Genesis 1–3 is written from that point of view. The idea of man created in the *image of God* is an idea about relationships; it defines man, not as what he is made up of, but by whom he relates to and how. The first effect of Adam's sin is a dislocation of the perfect relationship between him and God.

God made all things to relate to each other and to himself in ways that he determined. That means that the universe is orderly. We cannot see the full extent of this orderliness now because of the confusion introduced by sin. The disorder that sin worked is referred to in the Bible as death. Jesus Christ restores life by restoring relationships. Through the gospel we are able to see the real nature of the problem by looking at how God dealt with it. The gospel shows us that all broken relationships in the universe are a result of our broken relationship with God.

Jesus and wisdom

We can make direct contact with the wisdom traditions of Israel in the Gospel narratives about Jesus. We will defer close consideration of the matter until we have examined the Old Testament background to it. I have already referred to the closing words of the Sermon on the Mount.[1] It is clear

---

1. The Greek word for wise used in this passage is *phronimos;* the most

from the consternation which followed that Jesus was making a very exalted claim. He was saying that obedient commitment to him and to his words is the only way to secure a life which has ultimate meaning. The Scribes, who had become the guardians of the wisdom traditions of Israel, would have pointed to the fathers and to the collected wisdom of the nation as the means by which one learned to act wisely, and so find life. But Jesus did not merely point them to the whole range of the wisdom of the past. He confronted them with himself and demanded total allegiance to himself and his words. That is why the crowds were amazed 'for he taught them as one who had authority, and not as their scribes' (Matthew 7:29. RSV).

In a number of places we find broad hints to the wisdom role that Jesus was to assume in his ministry. Luke concludes his account of the events surrounding the circumcision of the infant Jesus by saying, 'And the child grew and became strong; he was filled with wisdom, and the grace of God was upon him.' This may seem to be a curious phrase if we think of grace solely as God's way of dealing with sin, for Jesus was without sin. But the emphasis is on the humanity of the Christ, and as such he received from God all the endowments of true humanness. Luke then recounts an example of this wisdom and grace at work in the life of the boy. As a twelve-year-old he amazed the teachers of the law with his understanding. When his parents rebuked him for staying behind in the temple, he replied, 'Why were you searching for me? Didn't you know that I had to be in my Father's house?'[2] In speaking of God as his father he claimed to be the Son of God, which we see in Luke 3 refers to the

---

common word used in the New Testament is *sophos*. As in the Hebrew of the Old Testament, so in the Greek there are several words which cluster around the same general meaning. In English we use words like *prudence, discernment* and *understanding* with meanings that approximate to that of wisdom.

2. 'In my Father's house' is found in RV, RSV, NEB and NIV. There is no noun in the Greek, which translates literally as, 'in the (things) of my father'. RV margin has, 'about my father's business'. It is clear that he was in the temple, but the emphasis is rather on what he was doing at the time when his parents mislaid him.

humanity of Jesus.[3] The temple is the appropriate place for Jesus to be since the house of God was the place ordained by God for meeting with his people. Jesus was thus perfectly fulfilling the role of Israel and of redeemed mankind to be the Son of God in perfect relationship with the Father. After this incident Luke again pointedly comments that Jesus grew in wisdom (Luke 2:52). Wisdom, then, is a characteristic of man in relation to God. He who is restored to friendship with God is, in one important sense of the word, the wise man.

If Luke is somewhat neutral in his references to the teachers who heard the boy Jesus in the temple, we find that he does not remain so. In fact the growing conflict between Jesus and the Jewish religious teachers is one of the themes of Luke's Gospel. These men become increasingly unwilling to accept the ministry of Jesus. In Luke 11:29-32 Jesus rebukes the Jews because they look for signs but are too blind to see the signs that are right before them (see also Matthew 12:38-42). By contrast with the pagan queen of Sheba, they do not seem to be very perceptive. The queen of Sheba was able to recognize the greatness and wisdom of Solomon and came to learn from him. But now a greater than Solomon is here and the Jews, who have all the privileges of the covenant and the revelation of God, do not recognize him. Solomon was always regarded as the big name in Hebrew wisdom, but Jesus outshines him by far.

In Luke 11:49[4] the conflict is with the lawyers and the Pharisees. The Pharisees are concerned to fulfil all the ritual requirements of the law, to tithe even the herbs of their gardens, but care nothing for justice and the love of God (verse 42). The teachers likewise weigh people down with the details of the law but refuse to submit to it themselves. So, says Jesus, they connive with their forebears who murdered the prophets: 'Therefore also the Wisdom of God said, "I will send them prophets and apostles, some of whom

---

3. The genealogy, or family tree of Jesus (Luke 3:23-38), follows immediately on the account of Jesus' baptism and the Father's word: 'You are my beloved son.' The family tree is traced back to Adam who is the first son of God. Between Adam and Christ, Israel is designated as son of God (Exodus 4:22, Hosea 11:1).
4. See also Matthew 23:34, 'I will send you prophets and wise men.'

they will kill and persecute" ' (Luke 11:49, RSV). 'Woe to you lawyers! for you have taken away the key of knowledge; you did not enter yourself, and you hindered those who were entering' (Luke 11:52, RSV). The point of this conflict is that these Jewish religious leaders so distort the truth of God's word to Israel that they cannot perceive the truth even when it is there in the flesh before them in the person of Jesus Christ. As they have persecuted those who in the past taught them the truth, so now they invite the pronouncement of this terrible woe upon them.

Since the traditional wise men, the Scribes, the Pharisees, and the Jews in general have shown themselves unworthy, the true wisdom of God is being withheld from them. In Matthew 11:20–30 Jesus pronounces a woe on the unrepentant and unbelieving cities of Israel. Even the degraded city of Sodom would have repented if it had had the privileges of God's revelation enjoyed by Israel. Jesus thanks God that the truth is hidden from the wise and revealed to children. He continues: 'All things have been committed to me by my Father. No-one knows the Son except the Father, and no-one knows the Father except the Son and those to whom the Son chooses to reveal him.' Here is a great mystery. Somehow the wisdom of Israel has gone astray and those who should understand it are blinded. In the wisdom of God the truth is revealed to others, to children, to the humble, even to those whom the Jews despised. And the revelation of this wisdom is in the Son. Luke 10:21 records this statement of Jesus in another context to which it obviously also applies. The seventy-two disciples are amazed at the effects of their preaching of the coming kingdom of God, for even the demons are overcome (verse 17). Jesus replies by referring to the overthrow of Satan, and to the authority given to the disciples to deal with Satan's power. These are the signs of the coming of the kingdom. Once again Jesus remarks that what is hidden from the wise (the traditional teachers of Israel) is revealed to children (his disciples).

There are many other passages in the Gospels which either refer to wisdom in relation to Jesus, or in which Jesus himself uses the traditional forms of wisdom sayings in his teachings. We will return to some aspects of these in

Chapter 11. So far we have seen that the Gospels portray
Jesus as the greatest of all the wise men, as the source of all
true wisdom. The Gospels also highlight the fact that the
Jews often failed to perceive the connection between their
own wisdom traditions in the Old Testament and the ministry
of Jesus. This, of course, was a failure which extended to
their perceptions of Jesus as the fulfiller of prophecy.

Christ our wisdom

By far the most concentrated exposition of wisdom in the
New Testament is found in 1 Corinthians 1 and 2. There is a
strong attack on *sophia,* the pagan wisdom of the Greeks, in
Paul's argument. The city of Corinth provided a challenge to
the gospel through its paganism and hellenistic culture. Paul'
meets the challenge head-on by showing that the wisdom of
God which is revealed in the gospel, is completely opposed
to the wisdom of the world. The idea that the son of God
should suffer in the flesh and die as a way of salvation was
stupidity in the eyes of the Greeks. Greek wisdom saw
salvation as a way to escape from the material world of the
flesh; it discarded the body for a salvation of the spirit.

   The gospel, the message of the cross, is the wisdom of
God for it is his way of restoring all relationships. But it is
also the power of God (1 Corinthians 1:18) because it really
does save and and because it confounds the wisdom of the
world. Worldly wisdom is condemned to destruction because
it declares God's wisdom to be foolishness (vv. 18–21). The
climax of Paul's argument is to point to Jesus Christ as the
wisdom and power of God (v. 24), and to describe him as
our wisdom (v. 30). The gospel is not a new philosophy that
rivals that of the Greeks. Rather the message is about Jesus
the God-man who is the wisdom of God. To understand
that, we need to know what Paul means by the gospel and
what he perceives true wisdom to be.

   The first Corinthian epistle does not contain an orderly
exposition of the gospel such as we find in the Roman
epistle. From time to time, however, Paul refers to some
salient aspects of the gospel. It is the message of the cross

(1 Corinthians 1:18). Its effects can be described as washing, sanctification, and justification (6:11). It is above all the message that Christ died for our sins according to the Scriptures and rose on the third day according to the Scriptures (15:3–4). Probably nothing is so distinctively Pauline as his description of the believer as being *in Christ*. This is a union with Christ in his life, death and resurrection. Although we were not around at the time, we, as believers, are accounted by God as having been crucified with Christ (Galatians 2:20), as having died and been buried with Christ (Colossians 3:3, Romans 6:3–6), and as having been raised up with Christ (Ephesians 2:5–6). In his life and death Jesus was our substitute and representative. We deserve to die for our sins and, when Jesus died for us, as far as God is concerned, we were there on Calvary dying for our sins in the person of our substitute and representative. When he rises to new life at the right hand of the Father he represents us believers. So, we are *in Christ* and *with Christ* in heavenly places (Ephesians 2:5–6). Everything Christ is as the perfect human son of God, he is for us. He now dwells in perfect fellowship with the Father, not only as the eternal second person of the Trinity, but as the well-beloved son fulfilling the role God always intended for his human sons. So Paul says, 'It is because of him (God) that you are in Christ Jesus, who has become for us wisdom from God—that is, our righteousness, holiness and redemption.' (1 Corinthians 1:30)[5] The NIV translation makes it clearer than some other versions that wisdom is equated with righteousness, holiness and redemption. It would be easy at this point to miss the meaning of the equation, especially if our ideas of righteousness and holiness are confined to purely moral concepts. This is another area we will need to consider further.

There is one aspect of all this that can be dealt with from the New Testament without examining the Old Testament wisdom material. Paul's view of justification, which is expounded in detail in Romans, is closely linked to the idea of the believer being in Christ. Our being in Christ is not

---

5. RSV translates: 'He is the source of your life in Christ Jesus, whom God made our wisdom, our righteousness and sanctification and redemption.'

some kind of mystical merging of our beings with the being of Christ. It is a declaratory thing, for God declares it to be so. It refers not to our state of being, as when we say that we are in some place or other, but to our status in God's eyes. It is Paul's way of describing the nature of our union with Christ. On the grounds of Christ's merits, God is pleased to regard the believer as possessing everything that belongs to Jesus. It is in this sense that 'Christ is our life' (Colossians 3:4). God actually treats us as if we possessed the very life of Christ as our own. In ourselves we are yet sinful, but in Christ we are righteous, sanctified, perfect. In ourselves we still suffer from the foolishness of worldly wisdom, but in Christ we are perfectly wise, for he is our wisdom before God.

The other aspect of our union with Christ is that it is a real union through the Spirit of Christ in us. Sanctification means that what we are in Christ we have begun to be in ourselves. So, if by faith we have died in Christ, we must also put to death what is earthly in us (Colossians 3:3–5). Clearly the moral dimension of sanctification is important. But we are moral beings as thinking beings. Morality implies responsibility, which in turn implies reasoning and willing. Moral transformation in the Christian is not separate from intellectual transformation or the renewing of our minds (Romans 12:2). Whatever wisdom is, we possess it perfectly in Christ. Part of our growth in holiness will be to grow in wisdom in ourselves.

Again, to anticipate the point to which we must return later, we see in other New Testament texts that wisdom is linked in very significant ways to the person and work of Christ. Look at the emphasis on the enlightenment of the believer in Ephesians 1:9–10: 'For he has made known to us in all wisdom and insight the mystery of his will, according to his purpose which he set forth in Christ as a plan for the fulness of time, to unite all things in him, things in heaven and things on earth' (RSV). Paul thus points to the intellectual content of the gospel as it reveals the ultimate plan of God. It shows us that this plan is much bigger than we may be used to thinking of it. Often we speak of salvation as something that happens to you or me or to each believer individually. Sometimes we get it together as the collective experience of all who are saved. But here Paul puts forward what we might refer to as the cosmic dimension in salvation. That is to say, God's plan, which he revealed in Christ, is to bring the whole universe or *cosmos* to its proper goal in Christ. The Greek verb here carries the idea of summing up or bringing to a head.[6] And notice how Paul stresses *all* things—things in heaven and things on earth. What may we learn from this passage about wisdom? Paul's purpose is not to define wisdom but to describe God's ultimate purpose. Yet wisdom is closely related to the knowledge of this purpose. Through the gospel we receive an understanding of the ultimate purpose of God for everything and everybody in the universe.

One specific side to this ultimate purpose is referred to later on in the same passage (Ephesians 1:17–23). Wisdom here is knowing our destiny which God's power will effect in the same way that if effected the resurrection of Jesus. But wisdom is not only God getting it all together at the very end. It includes also how the gospel enables us to engage in the task of getting things back together in our lives now. Paul prays that the believers may have wisdom so that their lives might be lived in a way that is pleasing to God (Colossians 1:9–14). Such wisdom is not first and foremost a knowledge of how to perform good works, but of what God has really accomplished for us in Christ. Likewise in Colossians 1:28, Paul links 'teaching everyone with all wisdom' with the proclamation about Christ. The goal is to present everyone perfect, or mature, in Christ. The same emphasis is found in Colossians 3:16 where to 'let the word of Christ dwell in you richly' goes hand in hand with the mutual teaching and exhortation with all wisdom of the Christian congregation. Wisdom and the revelation of Christ are the same thing.

One last reference in this regard is Paul's statement in Colossians 2:2–3. This passage demolishes any idea that wisdom is a purely intellectual exercise. Paul refers to his striving on behalf of his readers. He says: 'My purpose is that they may be encouraged in heart and united in love, so

---

6. *anakephalaiōsasthai.*

that they may have the full riches of complete understanding, in order that they may know the mystery of God, namely, Christ, in whom are hidden all the treasures of wisdom and knowledge.' Notice how wisdom is linked with mutual encouragement and love. Growth in understanding is to be found in the mutual life of the congregation. We should understand also the force of the word mystery. It is something which is beyond human ability to find out, not open to human reason. It must be made known to us by revelation from God. Paul could not imply that knowing the mystery of God means that we can plumb the depths of God's mind and being for he exclaims: 'Oh! the depth of the riches of the wisdom and knowledge of God! How unsearchable his judgments and his paths beyond tracing out!' (Romans 11:33). No, we cannot know God as he knows himself. But we can know God truly as he has revealed himself in Jesus Christ. All the treasures of wisdom and knowledge are hidden in Christ! Do we really believe that? They are hidden in the sense that we must search them out and know them. We can never know them all for Christ is true God as well as true man. But again, what we can know we can know truly. And if all the treasures of wisdom and knowledge are in Christ, think what that means for the whole intellectual pilgrimage of mankind. If it means nothing else, it means that all of man's search for knowledge is defective in some critical way when it is not pursued in the light of Jesus Christ. The gospel has a controlling interest in all true knowledge. What I mean by that will, I trust, become clearer as we continue this study.

I will conclude this chapter by suggesting a tentative definition of what it means to be the mature Christian that Paul speaks of in Colossians 1:28. A mature Christian is one who is able to look at the whole of reality through Christian eyes. He is in the process of achieving an integrated over-view of reality in those areas that belong to his experience as well as in those areas that he knows only theoretically. He is learning to understand all things in terms of what they are in this corrupted realm and of what God intends them to be by virtue of his redeeming work. Thus, he is an integrated person who is learning daily through the gospel how to relate, not only to himself, but to all things according to the creative purpose of God.

Questions for study

1. Look up 1 Corinthians 1:26–30. How does v. 30, a statement about Christ, relate to vv. 26–27, a statement about us?

2. What does it mean in v. 30 that Christ has become for us wisdom from God?

3. In Ephesians 1:7–10 how does the gospel figure as the wisdom of God, and what does it say about restored relationships?

3

The Wisdom of the World

Summary

There are two kinds of wisdom that need to be clearly distinguished. The first is worldly wisdom which looks at the world as if God were not real, and thus has not revealed himself in the person and work of Christ. The other is the true wisdom which comes from God, who alone can tell us what the universe really means. Yet in daily life we draw constantly on worldly wisdom because it works. It is based on human experience and involves the recognition that there is order in the universe. But when it addresses the ultimate or eternal significance of things worldly wisdom is opposed to the wisdom of God. Within the limited view of practical living, worldly and godly wisdom may coincide so that there is a meeting of the minds of Christian and non-Christian, of Israelite and pagan. But there is no agreement about the basis upon which we ultimately interpret things and events. The Christian's distinctive claim is that God the Creator alone can interpret all things in the universe.

The foolishness of worldly wisdom

'Has not God made foolish the wisdom of the world?' (1 Corinthians 1:20). It is easy to agree that indeed he has. But then we are faced with a problem for, when we think about it, we are absorbing, using and approving worldly wisdom every day of our lives. Consequently, we find ourselves asking in what sense the vast storehouse of knowledge gained by a sinful and unbelieving community is foolishness, and in what sense it is wisdom.

Let us summarize Paul's assertions about the two kinds of wisdom which he makes in 1 Corinthians 1 and 2. First, Paul says that the gospel would be emptied of its power if he were to preach it with eloquent worldly wisdom (1:17). This is because the wisdom of the world judges this gospel, the message of the cross, to be foolishness (1:18). Such wisdom is therefore doomed to perish (1:19). Worldly wisdom is actually foolishness because it cannot put man in touch with reality by bringing him to God (1:20–21a). God's way of salvation through the preaching of Christ crucified is an offence to the Jews and stupidity to the Greeks, yet it is both the power and wisdom of God (1:18–24). So, that which the unbelieving world calls foolishness is in fact wiser than the wisdom of the world (1:25). Paul avoids the wisdom which the world sees as superior and persuasive, and centres his whole message on Christ crucified (2:1–4). He does this in order that faith might rest, not in man's wisdom, but in God's power (2:5). Paul's wisdom is wisdom from God which is taught by the Spirit of God (2:6–13). He who does not have the Spirit of God will never see this true wisdom for what it is (2:14–16).

Paul shows us that we must distinguish between the meaning of things in a limited sense, and ultimate meaning. Things may be meaningful to us in the immediate situation of life in which we find ourselves. Elementary arithmetic is meaningful in the context of our society which is oriented to statistics, accounting and the use of money. But how do we relate it to ultimate questions of the meaning of our existence and of eternity? Paul speaks of wisdom as it seeks to embrace such ultimate questions as the way to find our rightful place in relation to the whole of reality. He is not saying that there is no validity in the knowledge of unbelieving people, or that sinners are as depraved morally and intellectually as it is possible to be. Rather he is pointing to the inability of human wisdom to bring us to ultimate reality and meaning, and also its inability to assess rightly what God says about ultimate truth. This failure of human wisdom is not merely an incompleteness or an inadvertent loss of direction. It is in fact a deliberate refusal of the truth. It is a dimension of human sin and rejection of God. The intellectual side of repentance is to be prepared to become a fool in the eyes of the world so that we might actually become wise (1 Corinthians 3:18–20). In other words, the gospel demands of us that we forsake the non-Christian views of reality and that we begin the task of interpreting our world in the light of the gospel. That is wisdom!

The wisdom of worldly wisdom

A moment's reflection will enable us to realize that, no matter how much we agree with what Paul says about worldly wisdom, we nevertheless constantly accept and act upon knowledge which does not have any distinctively Christian source or context. In everyday life it would never occur to us in most situations to enquire if some information we wanted came from a Christian or a non-Christian. If we want to know how to lay bricks or repair a lawn mower or even programme a computer, we consider it important that we get reliable information, but not that our informant be a Christian. We may seek out a Christian mechanic or electrician on the grounds that he can be expected to do an honest job, but his level of competence is not necessarily the same as his level of Christian commitment.

One of the more difficult sayings of Jesus is the story of the dishonest steward (Luke 16:1–9). In order to cushion the disastrous effects of his imminent dismissal, the steward alters the accounts of his master's creditors, hoping thereby to have some friends when in need of them. There is no question of Jesus condoning the man's fraudulent approach to his master's goods. However, he does commend the prudence of the steward in the way he pursues his own ends. We might suggest that, within the limited framework of this event, the man acted with some wisdom. He perceived the nature of his problem and he set out with cunning to solve it. When faced with possible disaster he did not bury his head in the sand but faced the problem squarely and worked out a solution. So, the children of this world often show greater wisdom than children of the kingdom of God in this sense, that they apply themselves to the problems facing them with far greater tenacity. Ronald Wallace comments, 'The average Christian of today is not willing to put into the matter of his religion even a fraction of the perseverance, patience and intelligent concentration that the man who knows only this present world gives towards perfecting his technical knowledge for his business, or even towards his hobbies.'[1] If Christians showed as much talent and shrewdness in the pursuit of the world for Christ as unbelievers show in the pursuit of riches, who could gauge what effect that would have? In ultimate terms the steward's wisdom is folly for he would be overthrown in the judgment of God. But in limited terms there is a valid aspect of wisdom in what he does. His shrewdness would need to be transformed by the gospel, but it is commendable wisdom for all that.

The general ethos of wisdom

So far we have seen that there is a distinction to be made between the limited validity of the wisdom of the world, and the validity, or lack of it, which belongs to worldly wisdom in its application to ultimate reality. The problem of the commendation of the unjust steward has similarities to the question of wisdom at large in the worldly sense. Most of us are aware of traditional wisdom sayings which belong to our culture. They take many forms, but the popular proverb is one of the most easily recognized:

> A burnt child dreads the fire.
> A stitch in time saves nine.
> Still waters run deep.

We know that these can apply to a variety of real life situations, and we do not discard them because they have no recognizable Christian origins. Every culture collects the wisdom of its people, much of which will be found in the

---

1. Ronald Wallace, *Many Things in Parables* (Edinburgh: Oliver and Boyd, 1955), p. 76.

form of concise proverbial sayings. In this study we will be mainly concerned with the collected wisdom of the Hebrews as we find it in the Old Testament.

Because the Bible contains a significant collection of Israelite wisdom works we are motivated to try to understand how such books as Proverbs, Job and Ecclesiastes came to be written and with what understanding of wisdom. Students of this literature have readily recognized that culturally the Israelites belonged to the wider world of the ancient Middle East. The discovery of large amounts of wisdom literature coming out of ancient Babylon and Egypt has generated much interest, particularly during the past fifty years. What is of special significance was the discovery of the close similarities between certain non-Israelite works and parts of the biblical literature.

Unfortunately there are always those who seem bent on proving that Israel's religion and literature are entirely dependent upon borrowings from her pagan neighbours. But in reaction to this pan-oriental approach to religion and culture we should not ignore the obvious contacts that were there. For example, scholars have long concluded that Proverbs 22:17–23:11 has close verbal similarities to parts of the Egyptian work, the Wisdom of Amen-em-ope. Did Proverbs borrow from Amen-em-ope or vice versa, or did they both borrow from a third source? Some have rejected the idea that Proverbs borrows from the Egyptian work because of what seem to be the implications of that for the doctrine of the inspiration of Scripture. But the last two chapters of Proverbs are attributed to authors that do not appear to be Israelites. Clearly, we must deal with the inspiration question in another way than by pretending that the problems aren't there. At this point we can at least recognize that there is common ground shared by the wisdom of pagans and that of God's people.

Our interest in Egypt's wisdom should be aroused if for no other reason than Stephen's reference to Moses as having been educated in all the wisdom of Egypt (Acts 7:22). Stephen does not suggest that Moses needed to repent of this or to unlearn it. On the contrary he seems to be saying that it was an important part of the preparation of Moses for his ministry. But we must remember the other side of the evidence as found in Hebrews 11:24–26. Moses refused to be called the son of Pharaoh's daughter and regarded disgrace for the sake of Christ as of greater value than the treasures of Egypt. So there is a good and a bad side to his Egyptian experience.

Egypt's wisdom literature is very old. We now have material which goes back to the middle of the third millennium BC, long before the emergence of Israel. By the time Moses went to school in the court of Pharaoh there was already a long tradition of wisdom literature. A lot of it is bound up with the training of young noblemen for effective statesmanship.[2] Usually the form of this would be what is now referred to as the *instruction*. Unlike the one- or two-line proverbs the instructions are longer compositions which address a pupil with directions, conditional statements (if . . . then) and motives for certain kinds of action. The Israelite equivalent is found in such passages as Proverbs 1:8–8:36.

An interesting feature of Egyptian wisdom is the place given to Ma'at. Ma'at was personified as the daughter of the god Re, but was never elevated to the status of a god itself. It was not a part of the official pantheon of gods and does not appear in mythology. Scholars have pointed to the difficulty in translating the word Ma'at into a satisfactory English equivalent, but suggest that it approximates to *order, truth*, or *justice*. It seems that Ma'at represented the order that was to be seen particularly in the stability of the Egyptian state. It was not merely a political or social order, for it involved the relationship of the state to the whole of nature. There is no real parallel in Hebrew wisdom to the Ma'at concept other than some similarities to the idea of order. These similarities between Hebrew and Egyptian wisdom suggest that the common factor is the quest for the understanding of order in the universe. Hebrew wisdom was distinct in that it was shaped by the Israelite experience of covenant and redemption.

---

2. An excellent introduction to the wisdom of the ancient near eastern cultures is found in William McKane, *Proverbs*, Old Testament Library (London: SCM Press, 1970).

Have we any real evidence that Hebrew wisdom was seen to have features in common with wisdom of other nations in the ancient Middle East? I have already mentioned the possible non-Israelite inclusions in the Book of Proverbs, and the contact between Solomon and the queen of Sheba. Other evidence also relates to Solomon. In 1 Kings 3–4 we have the account of his being granted wisdom. On the one hand this wisdom is clearly a gift from God, and on the other it involves Solomon's experience or empirical knowledge of nature. He speaks of plants and animals, composes songs and proverbs, and makes wise judgments in his capacity as king. Initially his request was for understanding so that he could govern well. In this there is some parallel with Egyptian wisdom. Furthermore, the narrator deliberately compares Solomon's wisdom with that of certain wise men of the East (1 Kings 4:29–31). Certainly his wisdom surpasses that of his foreign contemporaries, but there is no suggestion that theirs does not have the status of wisdom.

It seems, then, that we can propose the existence of a general concept or ethos of wisdom, not only in biblical times, but also throughout history. In theological terms, this general wisdom would be an outworking of the so-called cultural mandate. By this we mean that in Eden God gave to Adam care and cultivation of the created order, and dominion over it (Genesis 1:26–28). The fall has confused this clearly defined relationship of mankind to the world, but it has not obliterated it. Man no longer recognizes that God is Lord and Creator, but he goes on making greater and greater strides in his quest for knowledge and technical know-how. To achieve the goal of continual progress, as it is usually thought of as being, he devises more and more sophisticated ways of observing, classifying and reasoning. But what modern technological man does in a highly complex fashion is at its heart no different from what man has always done. He has observed his world and tried to classify his experience as a way of getting to the underlying order of things.

Atheistic humanity is thus capable of using the faculties given by an unacknowledged Creator, and of continuing to exercise the cultural mandate, albeit in a corrupted way.

Society establishes ethical frameworks in order to limit threats to social well-being that come from within. But in doing so it also rejects the prospect of a Creator who alone has the right to decree what is right and what is wrong. Conservation movements attack the doctrine of economic growth at any cost, and point to the threat of ecological disaster. The nuclear protest gains momentum because this generation not only has the capacity to destroy this planet but is in increasing danger of doing so. What was once seen as a political subterfuge by a small group of fanatics bent on control of the world, is now taken up as the genuine concern of millions of ordinary people. All these situations force Christians to face critical moral issues and to speak to them from a truly Christian perspective.

The point of these examples of common concerns is that they are *common* concerns, and there are many aspects of them upon which Christians and non-Christians will agree. This is because faith and regeneration do not remove Christians from the world. They will go on sharing the same humanity and the same universe until the end of this age. So what is the difference between a Christian and a non-Christian view of things?[3] The real distinctions lie in the way they look at ultimate meaning. By refusing God's revelation of himself in Jesus Christ, the non-Christian thinks of the universe as self-contained. Its meaning is open to our investigation. There can be no question of a God who is distinct from the universe and who gives it meaning. Unbelieving man often disguises his rejection of God's revelation of himself by constructing alternative beliefs about God or gods. But whether he calls himself religious or atheist, the assumption is that he can know things truly on the evidence of his senses alone.

World-views in conflict

The Christian rejects this assumption of a universe which is

3. See James W. Sire, *The Universe Next Door* (Downers Grove: Inter-Varsity Press, 1976), and C. Van Til, *The Doctrine of Scripture* (Ripon: Den Dulk Christian Foundation, 1967).

shut up against the God of the Bible. He accepts rather that
God is self-sufficient, personal, and in complete control.
While the atheist view of reality is a closed system of cause
and effect, the Christian view is a universe in which cause
and effect are established by God and open to his sovereign
intervention. We need the revelation of God in order to
know that the universe is in fact like this. We do not know all
the answers yet. We never will know *all* the answers because
some can be known by God alone. Because God has
revealed that the ultimate meaning of reality lies beyond the
ability of man to discover for himself, we know that
empirical knowledge is always in that sense defective. What
man discovers by himself, and what he reasons from it, will
never bring him to understand God and to know him. Thus,
we have returned to Paul's assertion that worldly wisdom
cannot know God (1 Corinthians 1:21, compare 2:12). The
Bible characteristically looks at reality in terms of relationships. Because God is the creator of all things, these
relationships must begin with God. To understand what it
means to be human we must know man as image of God.
The non-Christian can describe many things about man in a
way that is useful within a restricted framework. But while
we can look at man purely in terms of structure, chemistry,
anatomy and so on, none of these approaches can show us
the real nature of man. They do not provide a satisfactory
explanation of the uniqueness of man in the purposes of
God. They can never discover and pin-point the exclusive
trait of humanity created in the image of God.

From the biblical point of view, then, the definition of
man is primarily a definition of his relationship to God. Such
relationship includes dependence upon God who is sovereign
and self-sufficient. By putting man at the centre, the
humanist claims to give him his proper dignity. But this
assumption of the pre-eminence of man is a radically
dehumanizing one since he is not perceived as imaging
God. The humanist sees man's leadership in the world as the
result of evolutionary accident. The Bible describes it as
God-given dominion over the rest of creation. It is reasonable
to infer that one aspect of the image of God in man is this
dominion. This ruling function was intended to reflect the

absolute rule of God over all things. It was Adam's sinful desire to substitute his own absolute rule for a reflective rule; he wanted to be God. From that point on sin confused and dislocated all the relationships which God had established. But just as the image of God in man was not totally obliterated by sin, so also the orderliness of the creation, though confused, was not completely destroyed. The planets continue in their courses, the earth moves in a mathematically predictable pattern, life is sustained on our planet, and human society maintains enough order to survive and even at times to flourish.

Because the Christian view of reality begins with the Creator who has revealed himself to us, it is in opposition to those views which establish the nature of things on the basis of experience alone. While the Christian accepts his responsibility to search for knowledge, he knows that human effort, discovery and reasoning cannot provide a comprehensive understanding of the universe. Empirical knowledge, that which is gained by investigating the world with our senses, cannot include God or the meaning which he gives to the created order. But this limitation of empirical knowledge is not a hindrance to the Christian's knowledge of ultimate reality because the one Person who has exhaustive knowledge of all things has told us by revelation what we need to know. Through the revelation in the Bible we are able to know what God wants us to know of ultimate truth.

The non-Christian is in a very different position. He has rejected God's revelation of himself, and has filled the gap either with man-made gods or with himself as independent and self-sufficient man. He sees himself as autonomous, that is, as ruling his own destiny. Even when he is being religious he is simply disguising this autonomy as he worships himself in the gods he creates. Such is the position which we broadly describe as humanist. Having rejected the Creator who established all things in determined relationships and gave reality its meaning, the humanist is incapable of understanding the real essence of anything. No matter how accurately he describes man anatomically, psychologically, or sociologically, by leaving God out of his understanding the humanist actually dehumanizes man. Furthermore, the empiricist or humanist will claim to know things truly while not knowing exhaustively. In this he is inconsistent.[4] No humanist would say that things exist in total isolation from each other. For a start he couldn't investigate them if they did, for they would also be isolated from him. And there could be no such thing as natural laws, or complexities of matter, for there would be only random particles. There would be no organisms, no people to become humanists! Once we recognize this, we will see that what things really are includes their relationship to everything else. When the humanist claims to know something truly, he is saying that he knows how it relates to everything else in existence. In other words, to know even one thing truly he must know *all things exhaustively*.

We can summarize this discussion by a contrast of three positions. First, the atheistic humanist claims to know enough to say that God does not exist. This is a claim to know everything, for if he admits that he does not know everything, how does he know that God is not included in what he does not know? Secondly, the agnostic humanist thinks to avoid the problem of the atheist by saying that we cannot know if God exists or not; he may or he may not. But this is also to claim exhaustive knowledge, for how can he know that God's existence cannot be known other than by knowing everything there is to be known? The last thing left for him to discover may be the evidence that God either exists or does not exist. Finally, the Christian knows that he does not have exhaustive knowledge. But he knows also through revelation that God does have exhaustive knowledge and can therefore define for us what reality is. By the same revelation this God has told us all that we need to know in order to know truly. The Christian can know God truly. He can know man truly, and the created order truly. He knows none of them exhaustively, but he does know them truly.

The Christian in the world

It begins to look as if distinguishing worldly wisdom from

---

4. This is discussed in detail by C. Van Til, *The Reformed Pastor and Modern Thought* (Presbyterian and Reformed Publishing Company, 1974).

godly wisdom can sometimes be quite a difficult matter. I suspect that one important factor in biblical wisdom is learning how to master the distinction. The New Testament shows us why there is such difficulty. There is a real tension in the fact that we are citizens of a world which does not yet appear, and at the same time we must go on living in a world to which we have become aliens. The tension will show itself in many ways, but it is central to our Christian concern to live consistently with the gospel. Neither total withdrawal from this world nor total conformity to it is an option for the Christian. Unfortunately it seems that we often solve the problem by a rigid division of our lives into the Christian and the secular. It is not that we have no concern to witness in the world or to abstain from sin. But when we are involved in pursuits that seem to be morally neutral we easily think in a worldly way. Rather than muddle along like this, we need to see that the gospel of Jesus Christ gives us the only true basis for understanding all things in an ultimate sense: 'Heaven and earth will pass away, but my words will never pass away' (Matthew 24:35).

One of the lessons that this word of Jesus has to teach us is that God tells us by revelation what we need to know in order to understand as much as he intends us to understand about the nature of reality, but he does not tell us what we can find out for ourselves. We will see from our study of the wisdom literature that wisdom is both a gift of God and a human achievement. It is our task to relate our experience of the world, and our observations on life, to the things that God reveals in his word. In taking up this theme the biblical wisdom literature provides us with many pointers to what it means to be the people of God living in God's world which has become alienated from him by sin.

Hopefully as a result of our study we will be able to ask some of the right questions about the meaning of the gospel for the whole of our being and life. In a hostile world we are to be 'as shrewd as snakes and as innocent as doves' (Matthew 10:16). Perhaps one reason why unbelievers have scorned Christianity as a crutch is that Christian have made little effort to communicate a comprehensive Christian interpretation of the world. We have tended to carve existence up into unrelated parts, often under the influence of a pagan view of humanity that has infected much Christian thinking. This is no new thing, for the early church was troubled by it. A Greek concept of the opposition of spirit and matter challenged the Christian understanding of the world. Gnosticism, as it was called, said that only the spirit is good and all matter is evil. Salvation is irrelevant to the body since only the soul survives. The name Gnosticism comes from the Greek *gnōsis*, meaning knowledge, and it was by knowledge that the real person, that is the soul, was saved. Gnostics could handle neither the goodness of creation nor the incarnation. A new Jesus had to be constructed; one who was pure spirit and whose body was an illusion. The seriousness of this error is seen in 1 John 4:2–3 where John makes the coming of Jesus *in the flesh* the test of truth.

The paganizing of the gospel in this manner, so that the true humanity of Jesus is played down for the sake of his deity, is a subtle error because it can appear to be so 'spiritual'. In this materialistic age it may seem to be a healthy corrective to the rejection of the supernatural. But we soon learn from the nature of the gospel that we cannot save the spiritual by playing down the human dimension. This *docetic*[5] view of Christ, once it is entertained in Christian thinking, gives birth to some very unhealthy offspring. If Christ's humanity is not treated seriously (it does not have to be denied, just played down or largely ignored) then our own humanity will begin to seem unimportant. Salvation will be, as it is often described, a matter of having Jesus (a spirit) in your heart (soul), which means that you are born again (in your soul) and will go to heaven when you die (as immortal soul). The Christian who thinks like this has little to say to the unbeliever about the relevance of the gospel for the whole person and for the physical world.

Docetism also produces distorted thinking about the subject of holiness or sanctification. The human element in

---

5. Docetism was the name given to the view that Jesus was purely divine spirit, and that he only seemed (Greek, *dokein*) to have a physical body.

our Christian life is played down in favour of the life of Christ (his purely divine life) being lived in and through us. In popular jargon 'Let go and let God' sometimes means that huamn effort has no place in holy living. The believer in effect is not only being divinized, but is actually being absorbed into the being of God. The real distinction between God and man which was established in creation is blurred. So, to quote another popular cliché, the believer is only a suit of clothes that Jesus wears!

This distortion of the God-man relationship also affects the way we approach the Bible. A docetic Bible has no human dimension, no historical and cultural context conditioning the meaning of the words. The docetic Christian thinks it is very pious to treat the words of the Bible as conveying immediate spiritual meaning without regard to what the original writer intended to convey. Sometimes a decision is made on the basis of the assertion that 'the Lord gave me a verse of Scripture', when in fact what the text actually says has no relationship whatsoever to the decision being made. This approach is not far removed from the belief that no human word of the Bible is needed at all since the Spirit tells me directly what to do.

The biblical wisdom literature is one of the most potent antidotes to the destructive errors of docetism. It reinforces the general biblical perspective on the relationship of God and the believer. On the one hand it is the answer to the worldly wisdom which leaves God out of its reckoning. On the other hand it rejects the false spirituality which has the appearance of being godly wisdom, but which, because it leaves our humanity out of its reckoning, is not wisdom at all but rather the resurgence of an ancient error that troubled early Christianity.

Questions for study

1. Look up 1 Corinthians 1:18–30. What does Paul see as the problem with the wisdom of the world?
2. How does the world-view of the Christian conflict with that of the non-Christian?
3. In what sense can Christians learn truth from non-Christians?

4

The Refining of Wisdom

Summary

When God created human beings he gave them the task of exercising rule over the created order. God's word was the means by which Adam interpreted the knowledge which he gained through nature. Sin confused the process of gaining knowledge because rebellious Adam refused to interpret reality by God's word. God chose Israel as the people through whom he would restore true wisdom to mankind. Within the history of God's covenant with Israel, wisdom began to emerge as a self-conscious human activity. It related to the way the people of God learned to act and think, and to teach their children. Wisdom began in the earliest times but flourished under David and Solomon. Israel's wisdom matured at the end of the historical period of God's revelation of his kingdom. Once the full picture of the meaning of redemption was given in Israel's history, a greater emphasis was placed upon the task of responsible living within the framework of the fear of the Lord.

Man under God

No higher dignity can be given to mankind than that which is expressed in Scripture. Of all creation mankind alone was created in the image of God. Modern godless thinking regards man as the most highly evolved animal, a result of chance plus time. His rule over the other species is the consequence of the survival of the fittest. By contrast, the

Bible sees man as the greatest of all God's creatures with the
God-given task of ruling all others. The human scientific
task began when Adam named the animals, and ever since
then the quest for knowledge and for control of the universe
has expressed man's urge to exercise dominion over all things.

The Genesis account informs us that the scientific task of
humanity is regulated by God's word. Adam was not left to
discover the universe unaided. The reason is simple. God
had to reveal himself by his word so that Adam would know
God and know the universe as it really is: the creation of
God. There is no doubt that the whole creation is stamped
with the character of its Creator, but that is not enough for
man to know God in a personal way. When Adam sinned he
turned his back on the revelation of God in his word and in
his creation. So Paul in Romans 1:18–25 tells us that our sin
makes fools of us all. By suppressing the truth about God
which is there in the creation for us all to see, we render
ourselves without excuse for the rebellion against God that
is in our hearts. But even before Adam sinned, God's word
was necessary for him to be able to understand the meaning
of himself and his world. God spoke to Adam and told him
of his relationship to God and to the whole of creation.[1]

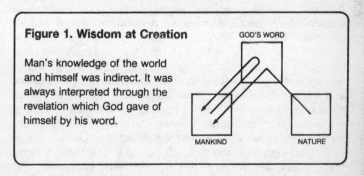

Figure 1. Wisdom at Creation

Man's knowledge of the world
and himself was indirect. It was
always interpreted through the
revelation which God gave of
himself by his word.

GOD'S WORD

MANKIND   NATURE

---

1. Van Til comments, 'Originally man's very self-awareness required
that organically revelational environment that comes from the interaction
of word and fact revelation. After the fall, supernatural redemptive
revelation must supply what the original word-revelation supplied to
Adam.' *The Doctrine of Scripture*, p. 66.

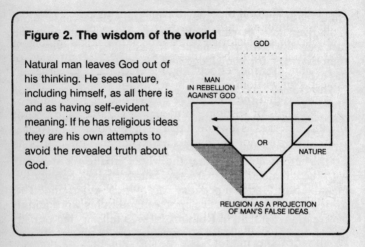

Figure 2. The wisdom of the world

Natural man leaves God out of his thinking. He sees nature, including himself, as all there is and as having self-evident meaning. If he has religious ideas they are his own attempts to avoid the revealed truth about God.

GOD

MAN
IN REBELLION
AGAINST GOD

OR

NATURE

RELIGION AS A PROJECTION
OF MAN'S FALSE IDEAS

Thus, before the fall, Adam's wisdom came from a perfect combination of supernatural revelation (word from God) and the discoveries of his senses. A basic principle of this wisdom would have been to accept the bounds of freedom decreed by the spoken word of God. Only thus could the proper relationship between God and man be maintained. Adam's sin was to refuse this relationship of creature to Creator, and the result was the dislocation of this and all other relationships. Historic Protestant theology asserts that at the fall the image of God in man was radically distorted but not obliterated. As a result, no one since the fall can or will acknowledge the truth of God witnessed to by conscience and nature. This suppression of natural revelation makes natural theology—establishing truth about God from creation —impossible. Traditional Roman Catholic theology distinguishes the *image* of God and the *likeness* of God (Genesis 1:26) and says that the fall affected the latter much more than it did the former.[2] Thus, with the image of God virtually intact, the sinner is able to discern truth about God from nature without the aid of the Holy Spirit or supernatural

2. The return to the study of the Hebrew text by the Protestant Reformers led them to observe that *image* and *likeness* are the same thing, e.g. see Calvin's commentary on Genesis 1:26.

revelation. Natural theology thus plays a big part in Roman
Catholic thinking and, indeed, it is a key point at which
Catholicism and historic Protestantism differ. It is important
that we understand how these two quite different ways of
understanding the effects of the fall lead to different
concepts of wisdom in the Christian life.

It is true that the tree of the knowledge of good and evil
has overtones of wisdom,[3] although it is rather the tree of
life that emerges as a wisdom theme in the book of Proverbs.
More important for our understanding of man under God is
the boundary set by God for the experience of man the
creature. By forbidding Adam to eat of the fruit of that one
tree there is no suggestion that the quest for knowledge was
forbidden. Nor did Adam need to eat the fruit in order to
know about good and evil. Obedience to the demand would
have established in Adam's understanding all that he needed
to know of the matter. The prohibition thus in no way
negates the cultural mandate but rather, along with every
other revealing word of God, establishes the only possible
basis upon which the mandate can be carried out properly.

After the fall, man under God is man under the
judgement of God. Sin has dehumanized humanity so that if
there is any hope at all it will be in complete dependence
upon God's mercy. This mercy of God is revealed along with
the judgment of God on Adam's sin. Although death comes
upon mankind, the grace of God is freely given in allowing
human society to continue. The end result of sin is death and
destruction but the finality of this is postponed. The world,
though fallen and often dangerous, remains a beautiful place
in which human life is sustained, at least for a while. This
common grace shown to the whole world allows sinful man
to continue to perform his task although he does it
imperfectly and corruptly. It also allows special or saving
grace to be shown to sinners for as long as God determines.
Those who receive God's word are thereby given the means
to interpret reality both as it now is—distorted through sin—
and as it once was and again will be.

3. L. Alonso-Schökel, 'Sapiental and Covenant Themes in Genesis 2–
3', in (ed.) D. J. McCarthy and W. B. Callan, *Modern Biblical Studies*
(Milwaukee: Bruce Publishing Company, 1967).

Israel under God

The evidence available to us of the intellectual achievements
of the people in the old civilizations of the Middle East
shows us that wisdom was sought after and written down
very early in recorded history. There is little doubt that
wisdom sayings of some kind would have been part of the
emerging culture of Israel's ancestors. Indeed, the pre-
history of civilized man referred to in Genesis 4–5 includes
the cultural elements of music and craftsmanship. If this
seems to be a rather non-intellectual wisdom, let us
remember that wisdom is a term also applied to the ability of
craftsmen (Exodus 26:1). It is not difficult to see how practical
know-how can be embraced with the more intellectual
concepts under the one term 'wisdom'.

Since the Bible is concerned with the subject of God's
saving grace, it is important for us to try to relate wisdom to
grace. The word grace first appears in Genesis 6:8 and
relates to the salvation of Noah and his family from the
deluge. The concept of grace is especially bound up with the
covenant and with the election of Abraham as the father of
Israel. The biblical picture is that God both revealed himself
and acted for the salvation of Israel in his dealings with that
nation from its birth. It would be a great mistake to allow the
lack of reference to covenant and to salvation history in the
wisdom literature to obscure the fact that the wise men were
men of the covenant. How wisdom and covenant relate in
Israel is a matter we will review later on. The covenant is a
specific expression of supernatural revelation. By this we
mean that it could not be observed in nature but had to be
communicated by a special word from God. On the basis of
the foregoing discussion it has to be said that wisdom,
without special revelation to supply the valid view of reality,
would be worldly wisdom and therefore incapable of
knowing ultimate truth or of leading us to God.

Israel under grace is also Israel under the law. The biblical
evidence leads us to say that grace precedes and governs law
even in the Old Testament. Israel was elected and called by
grace. Grace made Israel the people of God and saved her
from Egypt before the law was given at Sinai. Grace

operated within the sacrificial provisions of the law so that all who acknowledged that they failed to keep the law and threw themselves on the mercy of God, were forgiven. Grace operated in the promises that were constantly reaffirmed in the face of Israel's disobedience. And what was the purpose of grace? It would make Israel to be the centre of God's activity to redeem mankind and to restore all the relationships between God, man and the world; the relationships that belonged to a perfect creation. In the midst of Israel's history and experience of God's redeeming activity, an experience which included the giving of the prophetic words of revelation, Israel's wisdom grew, flourished, developed, languished and took some disastrous wrong turns, but never died.

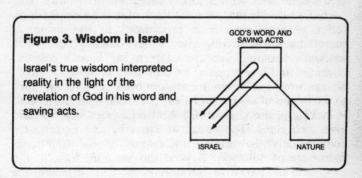

Figure 3. Wisdom in Israel

Israel's true wisdom interpreted reality in the light of the revelation of God in his word and saving acts.

GOD'S WORD AND SAVING ACTS

ISRAEL

NATURE

Wisdom in Israel

In order to speak about wisdom in Israel we have to make some assumptions about what wisdom is. Those books of the Bible that we refer to as wisdom books have certain characteristics which are more or less distinct. The evidence from Israel, Egypt and Mesopotamia is that there was a developed form of wisdom which involved more than knowledge as such. There are characteristic ways of pursuing knowledge, of putting it in writing and of passing it on. Set literary forms, such as the proverb, developed as suitable to

G&W-D

the peculiar aims of wisdom. Certain distinctive words recur
again and again, and these are not only words which refer to
the intellectual activity of man. But for all this, wisdom
remains an elusive concept because it can describe several
things. In the broadest sense it describes the thinking and
acting which makes for a truly human existence with mastery
of life. In the narrower sense it is a technical term for a way
of thinking peculiar, it would seem, to a particular group but
still available in some measure to the wider community. It is
a way of writing, or rather several ways of writing. In Egypt,
and possibly in Israel, it is a way of educating.

We should be prepared for the possibility that to seek a
definition of wisdom in terms of distinct origins, forms or
concepts, is to pave the way for an artificial idea of wisdom
as a single thing with a totally independent identity. But
even if we decide that we must think of it as an emphasis or
series of emphases, it is proclaimed in the Bible as
something worth striving after. I have already noted that
wisdom's apparent lack of concern for Israel's history,
covenant and law is one of its distinctive features. Perhaps
we can work back from the wisdom books to look for clues
to the origins of wisdom in Israel. The wisdom literature itself
is lacking in the kind of historical references which would
give such clues. The books of Proverbs and Ecclesiastes
contain only the briefest indications of the traditional
patronage of Solomon. Beyond this we must look to the
prophetic and narrative literature in the Old Testament for
evidences of wisdom in the life of Israel.

We may suggest four kinds of evidence which contribute
to our understanding of the history of wisdom in Israel.
First, there are the scattered wisdom sayings found in various
parts of the narrative literature of the Old Testament. Some
of these are clues to a pre-literary stage which probably
existed before there were any movements towards either
schools of wisdom or written wisdom. For example, there
are some instances of a popular, 'they say', type of wisdom.
We all know how a statement like, 'they say it is very good
for you', carries the weight of irrefutable wisdom for many,
although who 'they' are and what their credentials are is
never stated. The biblical examples are not always clear as to

their meaning, but they indicate the existence of popular sayings introduced by such a formula as, 'therefore it is said':

> He was a mighty hunter before the Lord; that is why it is said, 'Like Nimrod, a mighty hunter before the Lord.'
> (Genesis 10:9)

> So it became a saying: 'Is Saul also among the prophets?'
> (1 Samuel 10:12)

> This is why people say, 'Is Saul also among the prophets?'
> (1 Samuel 19:24)

> That is why they say, 'The blind and lame will not enter the place.'
> (2 Samuel 5:8)

In the case of 1 Samuel 10:12 the word 'saying' translates the Hebrew word *mashal,* which is the word for proverb in the wisdom books. How these sayings functioned is not really explained, but the obscurity of some of them should not discourage us. We can at least see that out of some specific situation there emerged a noteworthy point which commended itself as of value to the understanding of human existence. We need not suppose that the sayings were used merely to recall the original event, but rather that that event invited some kind of comparison with other events.[4]

Other examples of the *mashal* found outside the wisdom books include:

> From evildoers come evil deeds.   (1 Samuel 24:13)

> The days go by and every vision comes to nothing.
> (Ezekiel 12:22)[5]

Another wisdom type is the *hidah* or riddle, but there is no uniformity in the way this term is used. In Numbers 12:8 it is the opposite of speaking 'mouth to mouth' (face to face) and may mean an obscure saying. The most elaborate

---

4. See also Jeremiah 31:29 and Ezekiel 18:2.
5. See also I Kings 20:11. The word *mashal* is not used here, but it seems to be a known saying which is applied to this situation.

example is Samson's riddle in Judges 14:12–18 which, to say
the least, is presented in a rather curious form. Some
commentators have even suggested that the text has got
mixed up so that Samson gives the answer to which the
question must be supplied! In 1 Kings 10 the queen of Sheba
comes to test Solomon with 'hard questions'. The word here
is again *hidah* but it is not identified with any particular kind
or form of saying. There are other texts in which *hidah* is
used with the same lack of definition.[6]

The second kind of evidence is in the so-called wisdom
books themselves. Because of the absence of historical
references in these books which would help us place them
within a history of the development of wisdom in Israel, we
have to look for other clues. Even the ascriptions to
Solomon in Proverbs are sufficiently vague for them to have
more than one possible meaning.

The third kind of evidence is the relatively recently
acquired knowledge of the wisdom literature of Egypt and
Babylon. The forms and functions of this wisdom suggest
parallels to Israelite wisdom, but often the differences
between them are more obvious.

The fourth kind of evidence is the wisdom influences on
the non-wisdom books of the Bible, although this description
begs the question somewhat. There has been a rash of
studies done in recent times in which it is claimed that this or
that part of the Old Testament was either written by a wise
man or at least greatly influenced by wisdom talk and
thought. If we could be sure of the identification of wisdom
influences, they would provide some valuable evidence of
the place of wisdom in the main stream of Israelite thought.
We would see how the wisdom ideas, which in the main
wisdom books appear in almost complete isolation from
expressions of the covenant faith, have been brought into
organic relationship with that covenant faith.

What can we say thus far about an identifiable wisdom
movement in Israel? Taking into account what we know of
Israelite society, the evidences of early wisdom, the literary
forms and content of Israel's wisdom, the wisdom literature

---

6. Proverbs 1:6; Psalms 49:4; 78:2; Ezekiel 17:2 (used together with
mashal followed by a kind of visionary allegory); Daniel 8:23.

of Israel's neighbours and the possible contacts that occurred, we can propose the following situation.[7] Popular folk wisdom would have emerged at various levels of society as the expression of what people learned through their life's experiences. It is not certain what form the earliest wisdom sayings took, but the evidence does not support the idea that the longer sayings developed from the one-line *mashal*. In the patriarchal society during the period before Israel went into Egypt, education in family groups would most likely have led to the formation of sayings used in the training of children. With the development of the organized state of Israel came the recognition of men who could give wise counsel in the matter of running the country. Somewhere along the way the sages or wise men emerged as a recognizable group. It is not clear whether these were recognized as officials of government, religion or education. It has been suggested that the scribes later came to be the guardians of wisdom.

It becomes apparent that although we may be able to identify the distinctive features of wisdom, it is not so clear that it is a single phenomenon. Man is an intellectual being whose search for knowledge and understanding is pursued in various ways. We can use the word wisdom to refer to a type of literature that contains a wide diversity within the group. We can use it to refer to certain kinds of educational activity in home and school. And we can use it for a broadly intellectual activity urged upon all people.[8]

David and the growth of wisdom

There is nothing improbable about the role attributed to Solomon as the patron of Israel's wisdom during its heyday. We know the wisdom of Israel's neighbours predates Solomon, and that international contacts were a continuing factor of Israel's history from the beginning. How much

7. See R. B. Y. Scott, 'The study of the wisdom literature', *Interpretation*, XXIV, 1970, 20–45.

8. J. L. Crenshaw, 'Method in determining wisdom influences upon "historical" literature', *Journal of Biblical Literature*, 88, 1969, 129–142.

Egypt and Babylon may have influenced the formal development of Israel's wisdom is a point of discussion we will have to forego. There is some evidence that David also played a significant part in the wisdom of Israel.

David and Solomon together mark a climax in the development of Israel both from the historical and the theological point of view. It was David who really united the tribes after the abortive rule of Saul. Following the Exodus, Israel had moved through a period of semi-nomadic existence until the conquest of Canaan by Joshua. The conquest and the division of the new territories into tribal lots led to the period of the judges when the tribes were held together in a loose federation. A principal factor binding them together was the covenant and law of Sinai. The judges were 'law men' who, sometimes in spectacular fashion, led a wayward people back to loyalty to Jehovah and his covenant. The desire to change this covenant-based theocracy into a monarchy was at first a sinful expression of a desire to be like the pagan nations. It was a failure of nerve when political stability and national security were seen to be dependent, not upon trust in the God of the covenant, but upon a monarchy with a strong military basis. Eventually it was shown that a monarchy, when it was allowed to express the covenant, was not only permitted by God, but was in fact a divine gift to foreshadow the messianic rule of God's kingdom.

The evidence for David's involvement with wisdom is mainly indirect. In the first instance (2 Samuel 14) a wise woman intervened in a knotty problem involving David's family relationships and their political effects. The wise woman urged David to make a prudent decision with regard to his son Absalom who had committed murder. She flattered David as one who had the wisdom of an angel (v. 20), which is the same as the ability to discern good and evil (v. 17). In 2 Samuel 20 another wise woman was successful in bringing to an end the rebellion of Sheba, son of Bichri, against David. A disastrous schism in the nation was thus prevented. The wisdom here is not David's, but it appears that the reign of David was one during which the 'wise' were emerging as a recognizable group in Israel.

In the time of Joseph and Moses, the royal court of Egypt

had wise men with specific functions.[9] A preliminary form of statesmanship was exercised by Moses when he appointed wise men to exercise authority over the tribes of Israel.[10] In Deuteronomy 4:6 there is an important connection made between wisdom and obedience to the law:

> Observe them carefully, for this will show your wisdom and understanding to the nations, who will hear about all these decrees and say, 'Surely this great nation is a wise and understanding people!'

Joshua is said to have been full of the spirit of wisdom because Moses laid his hands upon him.[11] This is the most significant thing that is said at this point about the leadership qualifications of Joshua. This wisdom of Joshua would include the loyalty to the law that Deuteronomy 4:6 refers to, but it would also involve skills of leadership and decision making about matters not directly referred to in the law.

Thus, while wisdom went beyond the specific content of the covenant between God and Israel, it certainly was seen to include it. Here is the character of God shown in the way he ordered the existence of his redeemed people. The wisdom of God sets out the response of the people to his redeeming love. Reconciliation to God by grace, and striving to live consistently with this grace are both aspects of wisdom. But the law did not say everything about this response. Within its framework the redeemed Israelite had to express his human responsibility before God by making a multitude of decisions about situations that were not detailed in the law. The laws and statutes could not cover every possible contingency in life. Indeed, had they done so, they would have expressed a radically different view of man from the one they in fact do express.

Having said that, we must try to gain a historical perspective on the way wisdom and law work together. To keep the law was wisdom but the law was not exhaustive.

---

9. Genesis 41:8,33,39; Exodus 7:11.
10. Numbers 11:16–17. Here the elders are spoken of as receiving some of Moses' spirit. In Deuteronomy 1:9–15 they are remembered as wise men.
11. Deuteronomy 34:9.

Israel was given guidelines in the law by which to understand
and maintain relationships with God, man and the world.
But the law was never a substitute for the God-given task of
the quest for knowledge. The humanness of God's people
meant much more than doing those things that were
specifically stated in the law. The law did not tell Israel how
to develop the arts, but it did put a significant limit to artistic
endeavour:

> You shall not make yourself an idol in the form of anything in
> heaven above or on the earth beneath or in the waters below.
> (Exodus 20:4)

The law did not tell Israel how to pursue the science of
animal husbandry for the provision of food, but it did clearly
prescribe what animals could be used for food and what ones
could not:

> You may eat any animal that has a split hoof completely
> divided and that chews the cud.   (Leviticus 11:3)

The law thus gave specific directions and established certain
bounds, but it never interfered with the pursuit of knowledge
or the task of establishing man's dominion over the world.

Another aspect of the relationship of law to wisdom is that
during the period from Abraham to David, God revealed
the meaning of the covenant primarily through redemption
and law. First there was the promise to Abraham that God
would be the God of his descendants and give them the land
of Canaan. Then came the redemption event of the Exodus
from Egypt and from domination by a foreign king. The law
or covenant of Sinai was given to bind Israel to the God who
had saved her. What was begun in the Exodus was continued
in the conquest of Canaan by Joshua, and in the establish-
ment of an Israelite state. But this saving history was not
really finished until Israel was established as a unified
nation, free from foreign threats, and constituted as a people
under the covenant with God's rule represented by the
monarchy. This took place for the first time under David's
rule.

One of the chief lessons of the Exodus is that salvation

means freedom from alien restraints; freedom to be what God intends us to be. This is the freedom to be truly human. The meaning of this freedom is revealed to us in the nature of the kingdom into which God's grace brings us through redemption. For Israel the pattern of this process of full salvation leading to the kingdom was not completed until the reigns of David and Solomon.

There are some important New Testament principles foreshadowed here. Not only is Christ the summit of wisdom, as we have seen, but he is also our freedom. Only the Son can set us free (John 8:36). Freedom and wisdom are complementary sides to being truly human as God created us. We cannot attain to either freedom or wisdom until we are united to Christ, for to be outside of Christ is to be in bondage to death and to futility of mind. Furthermore, the law was given to tutor Israel until Christ came. Once Christ came, the people of God were freed from the law (Galatians 3:23–29).

The rule of Christ in his kingdom is especially prefigured in Israel's history by the reign of David. This is the climax of saving history as it is foreshadowed in Israel. The law could not pass from Israel when David ruled because Christ was yet to be revealed. But at least the freedom of Christ's kingdom was for a while foreshadowed with David and Solomon, and in like manner the wisdom of Christ's kingdom was foreshadowed. It is to be expected that once the process of salvation history in Israel reaches this critical point, the stage would be set for a flowering of wisdom. The tutelage of the law loses its absolute status because the kingdom means the freedom to live wisely and responsibly.[12]

Thus wisdom grew from Israel's beginnings, but during the formative period of salvation history it was not prominent in the life of Israel. The structures of covenant and law governed the actions of the people of God much more clearly than wisdom. There are two stages by which the law lost its tutor or 'baby-sitter' status. The first took place when there was a complete model of the kingdom set up in the historical experience of Israel. This occurred with David and

---

12. This concept of Israel coming of age is argued by Walter Brueggemann, *In Man We Trust* (Atlanta: John Knox Press, 1972), Ch. 2.

Solomon.[13] God wants his people to live, not by a lot of rules and regulations, but responsibly and in a manner which harmonizes with his kingly rule. The revelation of the kingdom is not finalized with David, and so the law retains its 'baby-sitter' status for Israel, while wisdom emerges as a new dimension stressing the importance of living responsibly. Thus, with the coming of Christ we have revealed the solid reality of which David's kingdom was only the shadow. The role of the law is now taken over by Christ in the gospel. But in the Old Testament the structures of covenant and law govern the actions of the people of God much more clearly than wisdom. According to the historical narratives, direct words from the Lord guide Israel on the path of redemption, and this is the preoccupation of the narrators.

Even in the period of the judges, the first faltering years of Isreal's life as a settled people, direct words from God and endowments of his Spirit guide the judges in the special task of nurturing the infant state. Gideon shows us an example of anti-wisdom or folly in his refusal to act on a direct word of God (Judges 6). His request for a sign and the putting out of the fleece show a perilous lack of faith in the prophetic word about the saving acts of God (vv. 7–10). That God granted Gideon his sign is evidence only of grace and not of the rightness of Gideon's request. Curiously this passage is frequently taken as a pattern for Christians seeking guidance, but this can be done only by ignoring its real meaning in the context of Israel's saving history.

So we come to David. The changes he effected in the structures of the nation's life, no matter how imperfectly they were made, reflect a profound theological shift in the significance of Israel's history. From a wandering people under the promise made to Abraham, Israel moved to become a settled people enjoying a measure of the fulfilment of the promise. David centralized the government in the city that he himself had captured from its Canaanite owners. He established a royal court and standing army. Most significantly, he made Jerusalem the focal point for Israel's

---

13. I have discussed this revelation of the kingdom of God in the Old Testament in *Gospel and Kingdom* (Exeter: Paternoster Press, 1981).

religious life by bringing the ark of the covenant to a
permanent resting place there. For the first time in her
history Israel actually came to possess, through David's
military conquests, territory which corresponded to that
which God has promised to Abraham.

If David is not portrayed as the wise man that Solomon is,
he is shown to be the one who made Solomon's leadership of
the wisdom movement possible. David set the stage for the
flowering of wisdom just as he set the stage for the building
of the temple. And David's son becomes the firstborn of a
new era. He is the master of the new freedom of God's kingdom, he is the builder of God's house and the pioneer of a
new age of wisdom. He is God's son, a prefiguration of the
Son who is to come (2 Samuel 7:14).

It is with David that we find a lessening of emphasis on
direct divine guidance. The counsellor emerges as someone
with experience and astute judgment in matters of state.[14]
Such was Ahitophel to David. There is no doubt as to
Ahitophel's ability as a counsellor, for his advice was 'like
that of one who enquires of God' (2 Samuel 16:23). But
when Ahitophel sided with Absalom's rebellion, David
prayed that God would turn his counsel into foolishness
(2 Samuel 15:31). This prayer was answered indirectly, for
Ahitophel gave Absalom the right advice. Absalom was the
fool for heeding the false advice of David's friend Hushai
who pretended to give better counsel than Ahitophel had
done (2 Samuel 17:1–14).

There has been much scholarly discussion about the
wisdom characteristics of the narrative in 2 Samuel 9–20 and
1 Kings 1–2.[15] This so-called 'succession narrative' may not
be the work of a wisdom writer as many claim it is, but it
does betray a new emphasis on statesmanship, counsel,
sagacity and astuteness.[16] As Adam was entrusted with the
world, so Israel 'come of age' is entrusted with the kingdom.
Time would tell how well true wisdom was being learned.

---

14. William McKane, *Prophets and Wise Men* (London: SCM Press,
1965).

15. E.g. R. N. Whybray, *The Succession Narrative* (London: SCM
Press, 1968) and Walter Brueggemann, *op. cit.*, pp. 29–33.

16. Psalm 78 may be added to the evidence of David's involvement in
the wisdom tradition. This is discussed in chapter 9.

Questions for study

1. Read Genesis 1:26–28. What does this tell us about the ground-rules for Adam's search for knowledge?
2. What did God do for Israel in order to re-establish these ground-rules?
3. What are the main sources of information on the growth of wisdom in Israel?
4. What characteristics of Israel under David's reign fostered the development of the wisdom movement?

5

Solomon In All His Glory

Summary

The biblical evidence supports the view that Solomon, despite his failings, was a key figure in the development of wisdom in Israel. God's gift of wisdom resulted in many expressions of human wisdom: 1. Solomon's wisdom had, within a restricted framework, common ground with foreign wisdom but at the same time was superior to it. 2. Solomon was capable of making shrewd judgments in difficult situations. 3. He had a concern to understand the natural world. 4. The material glory of Solomon's kingdom was related to wisdom. 5. The temple was the means by which the Israelite could make sense of the universe because it represented the activity of God in restoring all things to right relationships with himself. 6. The focal point of wisdom was the fear of the Lord, which meant faith in the redeeming acts of God. The temple and the fear of the Lord are closely related, and they give Israelite wisdom its distinctive trait. This is how the human pursuit of wisdom is tied to the saving work of God.

The dark side of glory

Solomon 'in all his glory' became a byword for the splendour that once had been in Israel. Jesus' comparison of this glory with the lilies of the field reminds us that it was quite literally a visual and material splendour (Matthew 6:29). There is nothing unspiritual about a beauty that is outward and physical. In Solomon's case it was closely related to his wisdom. But Solomon is a puzzle, a contradiction. It seems as if there were two sides to this complex man which the narrative writer neither reconciles, nor appears concerned to reconcile. No sooner was Solomon established as king than he made a marriage alliance with Egypt. In I Kings 3:1–2 the matter is noted almost neutrally even though it was a serious breach of the law. It is also mentioned without comment that, because there was as yet no temple built, sacrifices were made at high places. The connection of these high places with former Canaanite places of worship is quite probable, but the narrator does not refer to the danger of mixing pagan elements with the worship of God.

It is not until I Kings 11 that a negative assessment is placed upon Solomon's foreign alliances. The law against marrying foreigners is quite clear (Exodus 34:11–16 and Deuteronomy 7:1–4), but our narrator chose not to mention the fact until after he had told us all about Solomon's good points. The only excuse offered is that the king was led astray in his old age by pagan wives (v. 4). This passage presents a very dark side to Solomon's glory. His wives 'turned his heart after other gods, and his heart was not fully devoted to the Lord' (v. 4). He did not follow the Lord as David had done (v. 6). He built places of worship for pagan gods (vv. 7–8). God became very angry with Solomon (v. 9) because he had broken the covenant (v.11). In this way the narrator prepares us for the hitherto unthinkable: the division and final destruction of the kingdom.

If Solomon was the exemplary wise man that I Kings 3–10 seems to make him out to have been, then there is a warning in all this for us. Even a great wise man can fall, and the seeds of his destruction may be very close to those regions where wisdom means responsibility and risk. The signs of Solomon's deterioration were there not only in foreign alliances, but also in the raising of forced labour levies (I Kings 5:13), and in the warnings against turning from the Lord lest Israel become a 'proverb and a byword' among the nations (I Kings 9:7 RSV). This would be a reversal of God's intention that the nations should recognize wisdom in Israel because of the covenant (Deuteronomy 4:6). Even pagans will have the wisdom to see that it is the height of folly to forsake a God who has proved his greatness in the way he has led and saved his people.(v. 9)

Solomon's wisdom

Solomon's prayer showed genuine humility for he knew that he was not equal to the task of ruling Israel: 'I am only a little child and do not know how to carry out my duties. So give your servant a discerning heart to govern your people and to distinguish between right and wrong' (I Kings 3;7,9). This unselfish request was rewarded with the addition of riches and honour to the list of God's gifts. Very soon the gift of a discerning mind was put to the test (I Kings 3:16–28). Two harlots both claimed to be the mother of one little baby. How does one discern the good from the evil, the truthful mother from the lying, would-be baby snatcher? Solomon, by suggesting a 'just' decision—dividing the baby in half—forced the truth into the open. Mother-love was prepared to sacrifice all claims so that the child may live. A simple, direct and uncomplicated piece of applied psychology illustrates the wisdom of a true statesman. All Israel stood in awe of this decision because they perceived that God had indeed given Solomon wisdom to administer justice (v. 28).

The narrative moves on to tell of Solomon's court, his administration and the beneficial effects of these for the people (I Kings 4:1–28). This section is sandwiched between two important statements about Solomon's wisdom, and is clearly intended to indicate some of the benefits of wisdom. There is also an obvious reference to the promises made to Abraham (I Kings 4:20–21, compare Genesis 15:18–21; 22:17) so that their fulfilment is identified with Solomon's reign. Another remarkable passage (I Kings 4:22–28) describes the food provisions for the court and the size of the horse-guards regiment. In the midst of this is the statement that during Solomon's life the nation lived in safety, 'each man under his vine and fig tree' (v. 25). This phrase so adequately sums up life in the kingdom of God that we find it used later by a prophet to describe the future bliss of the kingdom (Micah 4:4).

The connection between the riches of Solomon's kingdom and the gift of wisdom is seen also in the visit of the queen of Sheba (I Kings 10). Notice the curious mixture in the description in verses 1–5. The queen had heard of Solomon's fame concerning the name of the Lord, and she came to test him with hard questions or riddles (Hebrew: *hidot*). Solomon was obviously an expert in the kind of wisdom known to this pagan queen and he answered all her questions. His wisdom and his material wealth together left the queen quite overwhelmed (v. 5). Again in verse 7 wisdom and prosperity are linked. The queen once more expressed admiration for Solomon's God who had so blessed him. Then the two monarchs exchanged expensive gifts. The narrative proceeds to describe further the opulent riches in Solomon's possession. 'Thus Solomon excelled all the kings of the earth in riches and in wisdom' (v. 23). And when the great ones from all over the world came to hear Solomon's God-given wisdom, they brought more expensive gifts to him.

How may we assess this materialistic side of wisdom? First, the material side of life is never down-graded in the Bible. God made matter good, and he has redeemed the material world through the incarnation, death and bodily resurrection of Christ. Secondly, the promises of the covenant were material as well as spiritual, so that the growing expectation of the kingdom included material prosperity. Thirdly, wisdom maintains this perspective of the goodness of creation so that prosperity is often a sign of wisdom. None of this means that prosperity always indicates wisdom or virtue, nor that poverty is necessarily blameworthy or the sign of a lack of wisdom. It may be that in the light of this evidence we need to redefine what we mean by the word 'spiritual'. It is not the opposite of 'material' as if matter were inherently unspiritual or evil. Rather it has to do with being rightly related to God.

There are some other aspects of Solomon's wisdom yet to be considered. In I Kings 4:29–34 it is compared with that of all the wise men of the nations surrounding Israel, including Egypt. This passage, along with I Kings 10, suggests that the comparison is not of the same order as Paul's contrast in I Corinthians 1–2. Solomon's wisdom is not opposed to the

wisdom of these sages, but it is greater than their's. They
recognized Solomon's wisdom and they flocked to hear him.
Paul's discussion is at a different level. He speaks of the
antithesis between the understandings of ultimate reality
which are held by the Christian and the unbeliever. He
would not argue with our narrator in I Kings who is
discussing wisdom at the practical level of life's experiences.
But, of course, Solomon outdid these men because his
wisdom came as a gift of the one true God who is the source
of wisdom.

What, then, could a covenanted Israelite and a pagan
discuss that could be called wisdom and about which they
could have some agreement? Perhaps there is a clue in
I Kings 4:32–33. As well as the prolific literary activity of
Solomon, there is noted his intense interest in nature, in
trees, animals and fish. This seems somewhat removed from
the matters of state and the discernment of good and evil
that Solomon was concerned about in his request for
wisdom. However, this is not the case, for we discover that
human society and nature are not separable into unrelated
worlds. Man and beast were created to inhabit the world,
and to live according to relationships established by God. In
a sinful world these relationships between humans, animals
and the natural world are clouded and confused, but they
are not completely obliterated. Wisdom discerns many
things about the world of nature which can instruct us for
life. Western man with his concrete forests, his manicured
lawns and clinical gardens, tends to forget how dependent he
is upon the natural environment. Solomon has much to say
to modern man about the meaning of dominion over nature.

The temple and the fear of the Lord

The narrative in I Kings leaves us in little doubt that
Solomon's building of the temple was a very significant
demonstration of wisdom. It is seen also as the high point of
the historical expression of the covenant promises to Israel.
God willed to be God to Abraham and to his descendants
(Genesis 17:7), not as a remote, impersonal deity, but as the

Lord of heaven and earth dwelling in the midst of his people
(Exodus 25:8). The tabernacle, and after it the temple,
would become for Israel the centre of the universe. The
Israelite knew that God could not be contained in this box,
as the Lord said:

> Heaven is my throne
> and the earth is my footstool;
> what is the house which you would build for me,
>   and what is the place of my rest? (Isaiah 66:1 RSV)[1]

But the temple was the place which was to symbolize for
Israel reconciliation, meeting and fellowship with God. In
that significant way the temple was the means by which the
Israelite made sense of the universe. If Israel's God is truly
the Creator, the Lord of heaven and earth, then the way he
reveals truth to be is the way it really is. Of course, the
revelation of God was incomplete until Jesus Christ, but
incompleteness does not mean that it is not true. What God
revealed to Israel was the only truth by which sinful man
could interpret reality, not fully, but certainly truly.

When Solomon had built the temple he held a great
dedication service which is recorded in I Kings 8 and 2
Chronicles 6. The ark of the covenant was installed in the
inner sanctuary of the temple, the holy of holies. Then
Solomon stood before the altar and prayed. As he did so, he
recounted the promises made to David his father that his
descendants would reign and God dwell among his people
forever. These promises were conditional upon faithful
obedience of the king and his people. Sin would have to be
repented of and acknowledged before God. What Solomon
describes in his prayer are the processes of mercy and
forgiveness that were already well established in Israel under
the covenant of Sinai. What is new here is the sense of
having arrived at a high point. No longer are they pressing
on towards the promised land or towards a stable theocratic
state. They have concrete evidence that the promises of the
covenant are in a real sense fulfilled.

Now the benefits of grace will overflow. When Israel

---

1. See also I Kings 8:27–29,39, 42–43.

recognizes the significance of the temple as the place where reconciliation and restoration to God can occur, it will be a people that fears God and enjoys the blessings of the covenant (I Kings 8:38–40). This great benefit will become known among the nations. Strangers will come to the temple and acknowledge God. Solomon prays that God will hear them from heaven and answer graciously so that all the nations of the earth may know his name and fear him (I Kings 8:41–43). The coming of the queen of Sheba was the first sign of this prayer being answered.

A couple of centuries later the prophets Isaiah and Micah were to repeat this hope that the temple of God would bring people from all the nations to acknowledge God. But for them it lay away in the future when God would act again to restore Israel from its troubled history of rebellion and covenant breaking. In these end-time days God would re-establish Zion, the mountain of the house of the Lord, and all the nations would come to the temple and learn God's ways (Isaiah 2:2–4, Micah 4:1–4). It is in this temple passage that Micah recalls Solomon's days when he looks towards the bliss of every man under his vine and under his fig tree.

But what is this 'fear of the Lord' that Solomon refers to in his prayer of dedication? It is clear from the biblical passages that fear in these contexts does not mean terror.[2] Rather there is a note of reverent awe. The biblical writers saw no contradiction between the fear of the Lord and the comfortable word 'fear not' which reassures the faithful that God forgives and protects his people.[3] There is some evidence that slightly different forms of the phrase 'fear of the Lord' indicate different origins and emphases.[4] In the period of the Exodus to Solomon it is faithfulness to the covenant that is in view. But we must never lose the sense of awe at the greatness of God who reveals himself in his marvellous works:

And when the Israelites saw the great power the Lord

---

2. There is a consistent use of the Hebrew word for the fear of the Lord (*yr'*) which is different from the word for terror (*phd*).

3. E.g. Isaiah 43:1,5; 44:2,8.

4. Joachim Becker, *Gottesfurcht im Alten Testament* (Rome: Pontifical Biblical Institute, 1965).

displayed against the Egyptians, the people feared the Lord
and put their trust in him and in Moses his servant.

(Exodus 14:31)

God showed his love for Israel in a demonstration of terrible
power as he saved his people from Egypt. Fear and trust are
the response to this saving act. On the one hand there was
the recognition of grace, love and covenant faithfulness, and
on the other hand there was a clear perception of God's holy
anger against godless resistance to his will.

After forty years in the wilderness Moses recalled for
Israel what God had spoken to him at Sinai:

Gather the people to me, that I may let them hear my words,
so that they may learn to fear me all the days that they live
upon the earth.   (Deuteronomy 4:10 RSV)

This fear of the Lord was to be expressed in their diligence
to observe the laws of God in faithful response to his saving
acts:

So that you, your children and their children after them may
fear the Lord your God as long as you live by keeping all his
decrees and commandments that I give you.

(Deuteronomy 6:2)

And now, O Israel, what does the Lord your God ask of you
but to fear the Lord your God, to walk in all his ways, to love
him, to serve the Lord your God with all your heart and with
all your soul?   (Deuteronomy 10:12)

Fear the Lord your God and serve him. He is your praise; he
is your God, who performed for you those great and
awesome wonders you saw with your own eyes.

(Deuteronomy 10:20a, 21)[5]

This concept of fear as reverence for God and his covenant
means trust and obedience towards the one who has shown
his faithfulness to his chosen people. It is inseparable from
the revelation of God in his word and saving acts. And

---

5. See also Deuteronomy 6:13,24; 8:6; 31:12–13.

therein, too, lies the significance of the name of God as the Lord (Hebrew: *YHVH*, from which is derived the name Jehovah).[6] The Lord (YHVH) is the name of the God who has revealed his character in the covenant and in the saving acts of the Exodus.[7] As God deals with his people and speaks to them his name YHVH takes on deeper meaning.

The phrase 'the fear of the Lord' is frequently found in the wisdom literature:[8]

> The fear of the Lord is the beginning of knowledge.
> (Proverbs 1:7)

> The fear of the Lord is the beginning of wisdom.
> (Proverbs 9:10, Psalm 111:10)

> The fear of the Lord is instruction in wisdom.
> (Proverbs 15:33 RSV)

> The fear of the Lord—that is wisdom.   (Job 28:28)

In Proverbs 2:4–6 the wise man says of wisdom and understanding:

> And if you look for it as for silver and search for it as for hidden treasure, then you will understand the fear of the Lord and find the knowledge of God. For the Lord gives wisdom, and from his mouth come knowledge and understanding.

There are many more 'fear of the Lord' sayings in the wisdom books, especially Proverbs.[9] The fear of the Lord is said to be hatred of evil, a foundation of life and a refuge.

---

6. English translations of *LORD* for the Hebrew *YHVH* follow the Jewish tradition of substituting the Hebrew word for 'my Lord' whenever the holy and unpronouncable name YHVH occurred.

7. Alan Cole, *Exodus,* Tyndale Old Testament Commentaries (London: Tyndale Press, 1973), pp. 20–22.

8. The phrase 'the fear of the Lord', in which 'fear' is a noun in construct, is predominantly found in the wisdom literature and the Psalms. The use of verbal forms is found mainly in the non-wisdom literature. See Becker, op. cit.

9. Proverbs 1:29; 8:13; 10:27; 14:26–27; 15:16; 16:6; 19:23; 22:4; 23:17. The verbal form is found in Proverbs 3:7, 24:21.

The question is whether the wisdom writers understood the idea in covenantal terms. I suggest that it cannot be otherwise. These were Israelites and, although salvation history is not a theme of their writings, they were not unbelieving philosophers professing a humanistic alternative to the covenant faith. They were men of God who reached out beyond the specific content of God's revelation and engaged in the search for knowledge and understanding of the world in the light of revelation.

How then did they understand the 'fear of the Lord' and its relation to their quest for wisdom? It seems reasonable to suggest that the fear of the Lord in Proverbs 1:7 is the climax to the prologue which introduces the complete collection that some editor has put together. Even if this were not so, there are enough reminders of the fear of the Lord scattered throughout the book to indicate the importance of the idea. The evidence, in my opinion, is that the absolute necessity of God's revelation for right understanding of the world was constantly recognized.

You will notice that the relationship seems to be double-ended. The fear of the Lord as the beginning of wisdom indicates that it is the point of departure. One must begin with the new mind-set given to us by God's revelation of himself in word and saving acts. Only this perspective will enable us to know the world as it really is. But then we see that the search for wisdom is to understand the fear of the Lord (Proverbs 2:5). In this case wisdom has the fear of the Lord as its goal or point of arrival. Perhaps this double-ended relationship can be seen in a comparison of Proverbs 9:10 and Psalm 111:10. Both are usually translated as 'the fear of the Lord is the beginning of wisdom', but different Hebrew words for 'beginning' are used. In the former the word is *tehilah* which properly means the starting point. In the latter the word is *reshit* which derives from the word for head. This word is certainly used for beginning in Genesis 1:1, but it can also mean goal or chief principle.[10] If this

---

10. E. A. Leslie, *The Psalms* (New York: Abingdon Press, 1949), p. 52, translates Psalm 111:10 as: 'The goal of wisdom is the fear of the Lord'. Artur Weiser, *The Psalms* (London: SCM Press, 1962) disagrees, as does H.-J. Kraus, *Psalmen* (Neukirchen: Neukirchener Verlag des Erziehungsvereins, 1966).

suggestion carries any weight it means that the fear of the Lord is both the presupposition or foundation, and the goal of wisdom.

We conclude that both the wisdom use of the 'fear of the Lord' phrases, and the traditions concerning Solomon as temple builder and sage, point to an important connection between the Israelite concept of wisdom and the covenant faith. This accounts for the truly distinct features of Israel's wisdom which, while it shared many of the characteristics of the wisdom of the ancient middle eastern world, never lost sight of the revelation of the one true God, Creator of heaven and earth.

That the saving acts of God should be related to human endeavour in the realm of the natural sciences, human behaviour, ethics, environmental care and social relationships ought to be no surprise. It comes as a salutary warning to modern Christians who frequently repeat the error of some early Christians in succumbing to a pagan view of the world. How little we have cared about the meaning of the gospel for our bodies, our physical world, our social relationships and political concerns. Perhaps we have been alarmed by the case of Solomon's apostasy. Was it that his relationship to the world became one in which all his past gains in wisdom were eroded as he lost sight of the fear of the Lord?

Whether we like it or not, wisdom tells us that there is a sense of risk to life. We should not be as the Israelites who grumbled about their new-found freedom, preferring instead to return to the safety of slavery in Egypt. Israel's liberation was not completed when the waters closed over the armies of Pharaoh. Not until David and Solomon did the drama of salvation history come to describe the whole process of redemption into freedom to serve the living God. But freedom entails risk in the sense that we face the uncertainty of all the unchartered areas waiting to be explored.

The fear of the Lord tells us that the risk of freedom in this sinful world is not fatal for the child of God. If Solomon lost sight of his covenantal bearings and began to conform to the standards of the world in statesmanship, religion and wisdom, there is no hint that he fell totally from grace. God does not ask us to go out into the world and risk losing our

way. Indeed, he has provided the means whereby we know
that we will without fail arrive at the goal. But he does not
allow us to opt out of being responsibly human; of using the
brains he has given us to interpret the world in the light of
the gospel. The fear of the Lord is both starting point and
the goal of wisdom, and in Christian terms this means living
by trust in Jesus Christ, the author and perfector of our
faith, the Alpha and Omega.

Questions for study

1. Read 1 Kings 3:5–14 and 4:1–34 and list all the aspects of
Solomon's life and reign that reflect the gift of wisdom.
2. How could Solomon discuss matters of wisdom with
pagans or have his wisdom compared with theirs? What
dangers were there in this interaction with worldly wisdom?
3. What did the fear of the Lord mean for Israelites, and
how did it tie wisdom to the covenant?
4. How does a Christian fear the Lord, and how does this
constitute the beginning of wisdom for us?

6

Proverbs and the Perception of Order

Summary

The appeal of Proverbs lies in its practical concerns and its apparently direct applicability to our lives. But there is a problem of how to apply it, and with what authority. The parallel forms in Egyptian wisdom, with their concern for Ma'at or order, suggest that order may be the universal concern of wisdom. The content of Israel's wisdom supports this. Of course, Israel's wisdom differs, to a significant degree, from the pagan concept. The concern for practical life and nature, and the absence of references to salvation in history, suggest that a theology of creation underlies Proverbs and wisdom in general. Two inseparable but distinct characteristics of wisdom are to be seen: it is both the gift of God and a responsible task for us. The gift comes not merely as an implanted ability present in some people, but objectively as the self-revelation of God's wisdom, to which the Israelite responded with 'the fear of the Lord'. Our task involves a response to this gracious revelation, and our use of the gift in order to pursue the knowledge of order in the universe. Proverbial wisdom is an expression of this affirmation of humanity.

The appeal of Proverbs

The book of Proverbs has a distinct appeal to Christians which many other books of the Old Testament do not have. This is partly due to its total lack of reference to Israel's history which would tend to tie it to events of Israel's experience. It is also lacking in any specific reference to the seemingly irrelevant, if not boring, legal material of the law of Moses. Christians have little problem with relating to the moral content of the law, but rules of cultic practice and of Israel's social structures seem remote and unrelated to our lives. For this reason Proverbs has the immediate appeal of dealing with life in terms that are often apparently unaffected by the gap in time and culture that separates us from ancient Israel. Because it looks at life without reference to the organized religion of Israel, and with a minimum of historical detail, Proverbs allows the modern Christian to feel that he can penetrate more directly to the essential meaning.

It is the thoroughly practical nature of Proverbs that appeals. Because we can identify with the more ethical tone of the material in an immediate way we do not feel the burden of translating the unique experiences of Israel, or its now defunct laws, into something which applies to us. The practical appeal is enhanced by the very form of the various parts of the book. Popular wisdom is characteristically framed in an eye-catching, attention-getting, even foot-tapping way to make it memorable. It avoids long and involved theoretical or philosophical discussions. Few of the literary units in Proverbs are more than several verses in length. Most are pithy two-liners, and some of these are possibly expansions of original one-line proverbs.

Proverbs appeals because it almost seems to invite us to use it as a lucky-dip. Each of the literary units, whether of the longer instructions (Proverbs 1–9), or of the shorter proverbial sentences (Proverbs 10–22), can stand independently of the others. We do not need to consider some specific Israelite context or some overall development within the book in order to understand any particular saying. Of course the whole book helps us to understand individual parts, but not because they are arranged in any given order.

A word of warning! The appeal of the simple, practical nature of Proverbs may be deceptive. We may in fact find that we have been looking at it in a manner that ignores the characteristics of wisdom thought and writing. Let me illustrate. In my childhood I used to enjoy reading a weekly magazine which contained a certain comic strip. This concerned an unfortunate academic named Bookworm Basil who walked around reading books of great learning. He would read some jewel of wisdom and then test it out. But it always seemed to backfire on him. In the one example that I can still recall, Basil reads 'Still waters run deep', just as he comes upon a swiftly running stream. Reasoning that if still waters are deep then swift waters must be shallow, he steps into the stream to cross it and disappears from sight beneath the water. The author of this comic strip may or may not have perceived it, but in fact he was pointing to a characteristic of proverbial wisdom which is deceptive. The proverb contains wisdom distilled from one or a number of actual experiences, but the way it is constructed may give it the appearance of being a general law of nature or rule of life. Ironically it is this apparent generality which appeals to us, and yet the proverbial form was never intended to function in this way.

The problem of Proverbs

The book of Proverbs is a collection of Israelite wisdom sayings of various kinds put together with little obvious order. Such collections, particularly when many of the individual parts are no more than single sentences, present special problems of how to read and understand them. If it is true that proverbial sayings are based largely on human experience, what kind of authority do they have for us? Wisdom does not come to us as revealed legal statutes or with the prophetic 'thus says the Lord'. Some wisdom sayings are overtly theological and even claim to be wisdom from God (e.g., Proverbs 8), but other wisdom sayings are simply human observations or experience.[1] Add to this the

1. R. E. Murphy, 'The kerygma of the Book of Proverbs', *Interpretation*, XX, 1966, 3–14, examines the kerygmatic or 'gospel-proclaiming' aspect of wisdom as it offers life to those who will receive it. J. W. Montgomery, 'Wisdom as gift', *Interpretation*, XVI, 1962, 43–57, proposes that certain parts of the wisdom literature express a view of grace that contributes to the biblical idea of the messiah.

evidence for the non-Israelite origins of some biblical
wisdom and we have what seems to be a real difficulty. It
may be that a rigid view of inspiration applied to Scripture
creates the problem for us. We need to remember that how
inspiration takes place is not the most important thing.
What we mean by the doctrine is that any part of Scripture
says what God wants it to say. We are concerned to
understand how the literature in question functions as the
word of God to us. Once we realize that apart from certain
reported dreams and trances, there is no indication whatsoever that the biblical authors underwent a suspension of
their human faculties while producing holy Scripture, the
problem is lessened somewhat. The empirical wisdom of
recorded human experience is not really so different from a
prophetic oracle, except that it lacked the prophet's consciousness that God was speaking through the author.

How are the various kinds of wisdom material meant to
function; how do they instruct us? One single answer cannot
be given because there is a variety of wisdom forms. The
one-sentence proverbs present their own peculiar problem
because they are not laws given by direct revelation from God
but rather are human observations from life's experiences.
Furthermore, the original context is not contained in the
proverb and it has the deceptive appearance of a general
rule. Therefore we must be careful not to use the proverbs as
ready-made rules for living. I suspect, however, that many
Christians approach them as if they were a detailing of the
ethical content of the ten commandments. This is an under-
standable situation because alternative ways of looking at
wisdom do not lie close to the manner in which twentieth-
century westerners think. Perhaps we can begin to modify
our thinking by considering the possibility that proverbs
function not so much to give us a multitude of individual
directions for right living, as to show us the way we go about
learning wisdom. Wisdom is presented as both a human task
and a divine gift, a combination which always causes a few
hiccups in our thinking.[2]

2. L. E. Toombs, 'Old Testament theology and the wisdom literature',
Journal of Bible and Religion, XXIII, 1955, 193–6, suggests that the
theological meaning of wisdom is found in the process by which wisdom
comes to man.

The forms of Proverbs

It is easy to see from the book itself that some nine distinct collections go to make up Proverbs. There is no logical or historical order to the way they are put together, and there is little evidence of editorial activity to produce the finished work. Some attempt has been made to gather together units of a similar kind, but this is not sustained. Within the two main sections of proverbial sentences there are indications of organization according to content, but this also is not sustained. The main sections of the book are:

1. Prologue (1:1–7).
2. Instructional sayings (1:8–9:18).
3. The proverbs of Solomon (10:1–22:16).
4. Instructional sayings (22:17–24:22).
5. The sayings of the wise (24:23–34).
6. The proverbs of Solomon copied by Hezekiah's men (25:1–29:27).
7. The words of Agur (30:1–33).
8. The words of Lemuel (31:1–9).
9. The virtues of the good wife (31:10–31).

The prologue is almost certainly an editorial note covering the whole of the book and setting out its purpose and basic presupposition. It highlights the distinctive concern of wisdom in the area of our pursuit of knowledge and understanding. Reference is made to some of the popular forms of wisdom such as the proverb, the figure and the riddle.[3] Lest wisdom be reduced to a purely intellectual concern the prologue points out two vital factors. First, wisdom concerns the young and the simple as much as it does any others, and thus is not to be confused with a high I.Q. Secondly, it is synonymous with knowledge, and begins with the fear of the Lord. In Christians terms that means that wisdom begins with repentance and faith.[4]

---

3. Respectively in Hebrew *mashal*, *melitzah*, and *hidah*. Unfortunately none of these words is used with enough consistency for us to be able to identify them with any fixed form.
4. See Acts 9:31; 2 Corinthians 7:1; Philippians 2:12; Colossians 3:22; 1 Peter 3:15; Revelation 19:5.

When we speak of the forms of the various literary units we are referring to how they are put together as well as to the kind of content that is typical to each. The forms are not of purely academic interest because a form will be chosen for its appropriateness in the performance of a special function. Without involving ourselves too deeply we can easily see the principles at work in the two main forms in the Book of Proverbs. These are the instruction and the proverbial sentence. The former is well represented in Proverbs 1–9 and 22:17–24:22. It was at one time suggested that the longer instructions represent a development of the early folk wisdom form of proverbial sentence. But this has been shown to be lacking in evidence.[5] Studies in Egyptian wisdom have shown close parallels to the Israelite instruction which are early and quite independent of the sentence wisdom.

The instruction

The instruction has all the appearance of coming from a school situation, although it may have had its place in the home also. The teacher addresses his pupil, or perhaps a father his son, and guides him in specific areas of life or in general concepts of wisdom. There is a typical form of the instruction involving the use of a command (imperative) supported by motive and consequence clauses, and frequently introduced by an address:

address	My son,
imperative	do not forget my teaching,
	but keep my commands in your heart,
motive	for they will prolong your life many years
	and bring you prosperity.
imperative	Let love and faithfulness never leave you;
	bind them around your neck,
	write them on the tablet of your heart.

5. R. N. Whybray, *Wisdom in Proverbs* (London: SCM Press 1965), has proposed that the instructions originated in Egypt and were extended to their present form in order to adapt the originals to an Israelite way of thinking, particularly about God. A detailed discussion is given in William McKane *Proverbs*. McKane rejects the theory of development from one-liners.

> *consequence*   Then you will win favour and a good name
> in the sight of God and man.
>
> (Proverbs 3:1–4)[6]

Sometimes the wise man praises wisdom, using the phrase 'happy is the man . . .'[7] This phrase is not confined to wisdom books as we see from Psalm 32, but it does come into the wisdom vocabulary in a way that suggests a hymn of praise to wisdom. In Proverbs 8:32–36 a combination of instruction and the 'happy is' pronouncement is appropriately placed as the conclusion of a long poem in which wisdom is personified as a wisdom teacher.

This speaking of wisdom as if it were a person in Proverbs 8 is a departure from the more standard instructions, but some features are retained. Wisdom herself summons men to be instructed. There is no evidence that the Israelites ever thought of wisdom as the Egyptians thought of their semidivine *Ma'at*. Personification in Proverbs 8 is almost certainly a poetic way of highlighting the important characteristics of wisdom as being both a gift of God and an activity of man. This passage has affinities with the poems in Job 28 and ben Sirach 24;[8] all are concerned with the place of wisdom in creation.[9] These are important passages for showing us how some wisdom writers came to think of the theological meaning of wisdom. They saw the universe as a wonderful creation in which each part was made to be in harmony with the whole. This orderliness of creation is the expression of God's wisdom.

While we must be careful not to remove Israel's wisdom from the covenant framework, its real emphasis was on the

---

6. The instruction form is seen also in: 1:8–19; 2:1–22; 3:1–12, 21–35; 4:1–9, 10–27; 5:1–23; 6:1–5, 20–35; 7:1–27.

7. Hebrew: *'ashre*. Perhaps 'blessed' is a better translation since it refers to the ultimate good of man and not to a mere emotion. There is a similarity here to certain psalms also using the word *'ashre*, e.g. Psalm 1 which is generally numbered among the wisdom psalms.

8. See G. von Rad, *Wisdom in Israel* (London: SCM Press, 1972) Chapter IX.

9. Ben Sirach 24 depicts wisdom at the creation, but concentrates on Israel as the people among whom wisdom came to dwell. This joining of wisdom and Israelite salvation history is a characteristic of this apocryphal book not found in the canonical wisdom literature.

orderliness of creation. The wise men no doubt understood that sin was a breaking of the law (Proverbs 2:17), a repudiation of the word of the Lord, yet they concentrated on a different perspective. Sin was foolishness, the negation of wisdom. It was that which disrupted the order and the harmonious relationships between God, man and the created universe. Wisdom was the principle on which the good life was to be built. The relationship of wisdom to law was thus an indirect one. Both come from God and relate to his character as it is stamped upon the creation. Wisdom sees the order primarily in the context of creation. Law sees it primarily in the context of the saving acts of God.

The instructions and the related poem in Proverbs 8 thus function to teach wisdom as both gift and task. They could be said to supplement the priest's instruction in the law. Thus, while the law says: 'You shall not commit murder', wisdom means learning from experience and wise counsel how to avoid the multitude of situations that could conceivably lead to murder. Likewise, the emphasis in some instructions on the danger of sexual immorality contrasts with the law's curt prohibition: 'You shall not commit adultery'. Experience teaches us that what is forbidden in the law can be observed as the disruption of good order, and as destructive of the good life. Wisdom learns from the experience of the multiplicity of life's situations so that we are better able to cope with their subtleties. But wisdom is not to be confused with the 'wise man of the world' approach to life whch must experience everything for itself. The whole concept of the instruction is that we learn from the experience of others, both good and bad. We follow the footsteps of the wise and avoid the way of fools.

The overall emphasis of wisdom is that we do not become passively dependent when we trust the Lord. Wisdom is telling us that not all of our knowledge comes from direct revelation. The fear of the Lord is the beginning of knowledge. That is, God has revealed to us what we need to know in order to be restored to a right relationship with God, our fellow man and the world. He has thus revealed to us what we need to know in order to interpret our own life's experience and the universe around us. Within the framework of revealed truth we actively go out in pursuit of the understanding of life, learning from our experiences and from those of generations before us.

The proverbial sentences

Among the sentence proverbs we find a variety of ways the basic form is used. In the first collection, Proverbs 10:1–22:16, many of the sentences place two statements side by side in what is called parallelism. The easiest way to explain this is with a couple of examples. The most common form in chapters 10–15 is where the statements make a contrast although not necessarily of absolute opposites.[10] By this means several key ideas are put forward in the context of real human experiences. Wisdom is set over against folly, righteousness against wickedness and so on:

> A wise son brings joy to his father,
> but a foolish son grief to his mother.

(Proverbs 10:1)

Another kind of parallelism builds on the first line by heightening its meaning in the second:

> Grey hair is a crown of splendour;
> it is attained by a righteous life.

(Proverbs 16:31)

Perhaps the most frequently achieved effect of the simple proverb is that of grouping. We often find different things placed together in a way that does not tell us why they are so grouped. No specific relationship is indicated in the way they were written in the original Hebrew text. For some reason the English translations almost always reconstruct such sentences into comparisons or into subject-predicate sentences.[11] Thus the NIV translates Proverbs 12:1a as:

> Whoever loves discipline, loves knowledge.

---

10. G. von Rad, *Wisdom in Israel*, p. 28.
11. A subject-predicate sentence makes a statement about the subject.

The Hebrew actually puts it in the ambiguous form:

> Loving knowledge, loving discipline.[12]

The effect is to establish a group of things belonging together, rather than to predicate something, that is make a statement, about one of them in the terms of the other. There is no indication of cause or effect or any other relationship between them. Thus there is room for interpretation which would not be allowed otherwise. The possibilities of this arrangement in a more complex form can be seen in those sentences which double the grouping so that A goes with B, C goes with D, and also AB goes with CD. For example, the Hebrew of Proverbs 17:19 has this form:

> Loving sin (A), loving strife (B),
> making high his gate (C), seeking destruction (D).

The NIV assumes a particular relationship between the two halves of each line. This reduces the possible range of interpretations:

> He who loves a quarrel, loves sin;
> he who builds a high gate invites destruction.

Other sentences of a similar kind have also undergone transformation in the process of translation into the English versions. For example, Proverbs 25:3, 20, 25; 26:3, 7, 9, 10, 14 all simply place things side by side with a conjunctive 'and' between them:

> Cold water to a thirsty soul,
> and good news from a far country.

But the English versions supply 'as . . . so' or 'like . . . so is':

> Like cold water to a weary soul
> is good news from a distant land.

(Proverbs 25:25)

---

12. See also 13:3a; 14:2a. These characteristics are discussed in detail in H.-J. Hermission, *Studien zur israelitischen Spruchweisheit* (Neukirchen-Vluyn: Neukirchener Verlag, 1968).

Then there are sentences such as Proverbs 25:11,12,13,14, 18,19,26 which place the things together without even 'and' to link them. Again the English versions supply the words necessary to build a subject-predicate sentence. This is not useless information, for the forms of these proverbs in the Hebrew help us to understand how they function in teaching wisdom. The English versions are tending to obscure that function. The wise men were not giving us general rules for ethical conduct. Nor were they defining unknowns in terms of known things. Rather they were saying that experience shows us that A and B have something in common, as do C and D. This is a form of perception of reality to which the simple proverb is admirably suited and our English versions have not, on the whole, helped us to see it. By removing the experience from its specific, concrete event the sages were not wanting to construct timeless rules, but rather to express a view of reality which demands a measure of our intellectual engagement. Thus two quite opposite (or apparently so) observations can be offered without the suggestion of inconsistency or even stupidity:

> Do not answer a fool according to his folly,
> or you will be like him yourself.

> Answer a fool according to his folly,
> or he will be wise in his own eyes.

(Proverbs 26:4–5)

The editor of this section may or may not have placed these two contrary words together out of a sense of the humour of the situation. It is clear that no contradiction is implied, but contradiction would have been unavoidable if these had been legal precepts or timeless rules. We must suppose that the interpretation is open-ended in that we are invited to supply the concrete possibilities for each. Some situations call for silence in the company of a fool, others for his rebuke. I found similar illustrations of this principle in a collection of Yiddish proverbs which produced the following 'contradictions':

> A friend you get for nothing, an enemy has to be bought.
> A friend you have to buy, enemies you get for nothing.

> Sleep is a thief.
> Sleep is the best doctor.[13]

Although they are different in form, the so-called numerical sayings seem to have the same function as these grouping proverbs. The numerical sayings use a formula of numbers n-1, followed by n, thus:

> Under three things the earth trembles,
> under four it cannot bear up.
>
> (Proverbs 30:21)[14]

Other numerical sayings occur in Proverbs 6:16–19; 30:15–16, 18–19, 21–23, 24–28 (which does not use n-1), 29–31. These sayings contain the element of surprise in the listings which come almost as if they were the answer to a riddle: 'What are three things under which the earth trembles? . . .'[15] It is possible that the n-1, n formula is a way of pointing to the open-ended nature of the list, thus inviting the perceptive person to supply further items n+1, n+2 and so on.

Miscellaneous sayings

The book of Proverbs contains a few sayings which do not fit into the two main categories. Two of these (6:6–11 and 24:30–34) could be described as object lessons. In the former, nature provides a lesson from the industry of the ant, which leads to a popular saying about laziness and poverty:

> A little sleep, a little slumber,
> a little folding of the hands to rest—
> and poverty will come on you like a bandit,
> and scarcity like an armed man.

---

13. F. Kogos, *One Thousand and One Yiddish Proverbs* (New York: Citadel Press, 1970).

14. Compare the use in Amos 1:3–2:8. In Proverbs the higher number is actually filled out with a list of items corresponding to it. There is no such relationship of the sins which Amos ennumerates and the 3, 4 formula.

15. So von Rad, *Wisdom in Israel*, p. 35f.

The same popular saying is evoked in the second passage by the observation of the run-down property of a lazy farmer. I suggest that here we have an illustration of the way the principle of open-ended interpretation operates. The proverb would normally stand on its own waiting to be applied to a suitable concrete situation. Here we are given two such situations which show how the same proverb is employed to assess the meaning of different but meaningfully related situations.

Learning wisdom from Proverbs

Despite its many cautions, Proverbs is an optimistic book. Wisdom and life are within our grasp because both are the gifts of God. Yet the gift is never without the task. The fear of the Lord is the beginning of knowledge and wisdom, and it speaks eloquently of God's saving grace shown to his covenant people. The young men and the simple, unsophisticated person can learn wisdom, but only if they would know the fear of the Lord. Proverbs is optimistic because God is the God of the covenant of grace. He gives good things to his children, and the greatest of his gifts is life.

Proverbs defines goodness in terms that are wider than morality and ethics. It is the order that underlies the creation. When God made the heavens and the earth and everything in them he made them in relation to one another, and all was good (Genesis 1:31). All was harmony according to the wisdom of God. Proverbs does not speak of the fall of man into sin, but the fall is everywhere implied. Wisdom, righteousness and life are in conflict with folly, wickedness and death. But despite this intrusion into the good order of God's universe, the order is not destroyed. The fool is the unredeemed sinner who says there is no God (Psalms 14:1; 53:1), who sees the universe as the result of blind chance. Yet, although he refuses to acknowledge a personal, all-wise Creator, he cannot ignore the order that is perceptible in the universe. He has no explanation for it, nor for the disruption of the order of which he himself is a living example along with all other sinners. The wise man fears the Lord and, unlike the fool, is in touch with reality.

Thus, in their distinctive way the wise men of Israel looked at what it meant to be in a disrupted order while not conforming to the disruption. The wise man had to learn to relate to God, to his fellow man, and the whole created order. But in so doing he had to learn that order was complicated by the intrusion of sinful chaos. The optimism of Proverbs is that chaos has not conquered, and that order can still be perceived.

Proverbs affirms the humanity of the wise. He who fears the Lord is not one who retreats into some fake spirituality. Wisdom saw that life is for living to the full. The man of God recognizes that his true humanity lies in his relation to God. But because God made us to relate to one another and to the universe, the restoration of a right relation to God implies a restoration of all relationships. We are encouraged to accept the tasks given to Adam in Eden which, though now confused by sin, are still open to us. In the course of our exercising of dominion in the earth a huge number of impressions are made on our senses which go to make up our experience. Dominion is not a matter of obeying legal precepts in every area of human decision. If we read Proverbs as a miscellany of legal precepts we might find that now and then a saying will occur to us as relevant to our present situation. Indeed we can see some broad principles of morality and behaviour in wisdom writings, but more to the point, we find that we are invited by the wise men to join them in developing a view of reality as a whole. Proverbial wisdom calls us to a decision to stand either with the wise man or the fool; to see all of life in the light of God's revelation of himself or to persist in the folly of making ourselves the centre of the universe.

How then is our humanness affirmed? Wisdom tells us that God has spoken and acted with sufficient clarity for us to perceive the nature of reality when we humble ourselves before a gracious God. God will not enter into our lives to do our thinking for us. He shows trust in us by giving us the equipment and then leaving us to learn about life. All of the collections, lists and comparisons in Proverbs are saying to us that it is certainly complex out there in the world, but it is not chaos. God has not withdrawn all his creative cohesion from the universe. Everywhere in the world around us are the evidences of God's maintenance of order if we would only see them. The wise men did not reduce all this to abstract statements as a modern philosopher might or as we are inclined to do. Rather they were content to observe life and to note that even the most unlikely things and events are related in some way.

For the Israelite whose history was one dominated by the consciousness of election, of the redeeming acts of God, of the law of Moses, and of the radical distinction between Israel and the nations, wisdom had an important function. The exclusivism of Israel's law which forbade what we would regard as normal relationships with other nations, had to be qualified both for practical and theological reasons. In the first instance Israel reached the zenith of its consciousness of election under David's rule. From then on it had to learn to live in such a way that acknowledged that it was in the wider world without compromising the sense of being the elect nation. Theologically Israel would have to come to terms with its role in the world as the agent of God's blessing to the gentiles. History and prophetic word showed that this role would not be truly activated until the Lord's great day of salvation, but, in the meantime, the world was still there and could not be ignored. It was not always the religiously inclined in Israel who perceived the wise relationships with sinners and gentiles. Jesus, as the very wisdom of God incarnate, fulfilled Israel's role to gentiles, but his contact with those who needed salvation caused the religious to scorn him for mixing with publicans and sinners. Being religious and fearing the Lord are clearly not necessarily the same thing.

Questions for study

1. Read one of the instructions, for example Proverbs 3:1–10, and a sentence such as Proverbs 10:1. Do you see any points of contact between them? What are the main differences in the content of each, and in the way it is conveyed?

2. Read Proverbs 10–11 and list some of the practical issues

or topics that are dealt with. Note how many proverbs (or how few) specifically mention God.

3. What are the main types of wisdom saying found in Proverbs, and how do they function?

4. What assumptions about the orderliness of the universe are evident in Proverbs?

7

Job and the Hiddenness of Order

Summary

The subject of the book of Job has been described in various ways. These include the problem of suffering, theodicy or justification of the mysterious ways of God, the meaning of faith, and the nature of fellowship between man and God. All of these suggestions have something to contribute to our understanding of Job. But, above all, the book is asking the question about the nature of wisdom and where it can be found. It achieves this by portraying the crisis which occurs when two concepts of wisdom come into conflict. The book expresses rebellion against a rigid understanding of the relationship between actions and their consequences. Specific observations of relationships are thus turned into general rules which then clash with further experience. Job recognizes that the order of the universe is not fully open to observation. Thus the book urges trust in God because he is above the order perceived by human beings and is not bound by it. It is this hiddenness of order which leads Job to perceive dimly our need for a mediator between us and God, whose word we must hear if we are to live.

The purpose of Job

Reading the book of Job for the first time can leave one somewhat overawed. Ours is the age of snappy communications, of the one-word bill-board advertisement, of the twenty-second TV commercial. Job belongs to an entirely

different world. But it is there in the Bible, and its forty-two
chapters have a message for us today. Because of the danger
of becoming bogged down in the seemingly endless verbiage
of Job, it helps to be acquainted with the way the book is put
together.

The book of Job begins with the familiar prose story of the
testing of Job's righteousness by the adversary (the satan).[1]
The rather surprising fact that the satan is allowed into the
presence of God raises the question of his identity. He is an
intruder, and he comes as the adversary of the righteous
man of God. He challenges the main assertion of the
opening passage, namely that Job is a righteous man. But
once this challenge is given effect in the attacks on Job's
possessions and person the book has no more interest in the
satan. If the book were primarily concerned with the
problem of why righteous people suffer it would be a simple
matter to say, 'Satan is getting at Job'. In fact, no such
solution occurs to the writer and, surprisingly, the satan is
irrelevant to the main discussion.

When Job is first stricken with tragedy and loss it is
emphasized that he remains a righteous man (2:10). Then
his three friends appear and, after a discreet period of
silence, begin their arguments. We enter now the section of
the book which is written in poetry. Hebrew poetry does not
work by the same rules as English poetry and this tends to
make it difficult for the reader who is not used to it. To us it
seems very wordy and repetitious. It uses the device of parallelism which we noted as characteristic of the proverbial
wisdom sentences. Actually, parallelism can be of help to us
when an obscure line is repeated in different and more
familiar terms. However, the real difficulty lies not in the
meaning of the individual lines but in the way the argument
is pursued.

The book has a simple enough structure. Following the
prose introduction the poetic sections begin with Job cursing

---

1. The Hebrew word *satan* means the adversary or accuser. It cannot
be assumed that it is here used for the personal name for the devil. In the
New Testament the devil is called Satan because he is *the* adversary above
all others. The adversary is seen also in Zechariah 3:1, Psalm 109:6, and in
a number of narrative passages.

the day he was born. This leads to the rounds of dialogue between Job and his three friends in turn: Job–Eliphaz, Job–Bildad, Job–Zophar (chapters 3–31). The sequence occurs three times except that in the third round Zophar does not appear. The last speech of Job in response to Bildad is exceptionally long (chapters 26–31), although the poem about wisdom in chapter 28 may be a later insertion into the book. A fourth friend, Elihu, arrives on the scene, but seems to add little to the arguments of the other three (32–37). Then the silence of God is broken as he speaks to Job in a magnificent poetic climax (38:1–42:6). Finally a brief prose epilogue has Job restored in wealth, family and health.

Many regard Job as a composite book. For example, it is frequently asserted that the original book consisted of the prose sections alone (1:1–2:13 and 42:7–17). These were then brought together with the dialogue and, probably later, the wisdom poem and the Elihu speeches added.[2] For our purposes it is the finished book in its present form which is of interest, for it is this which has come down to us as holy Scripture and which stands as one of the literary classics of all time.

It can hardly be denied that a central theme of the book is the suffering of a righteous man. That is not necessarily to say that the purpose of the book is to give an answer to the problem of the righteous suffering. The very length and form of the book seem to increase the sense of oppressive mystery surrounding Job's suffering. From one point of view the problem does not exist for we know from the opening narrative that God approves of Job and confidently allows the genuineness of his faith to be tested. But this dialogue between God and the satan is something that we know but that Job does not. This ignorance on Job's part of the true situation gives continuity between the prose story and the great poetic dialogues with the friends. Scripture supports the idea that God allows suffering among his people in order to chastise and correct them.[3] Also, Job's righteousness did

---

2. The composition of the book is discussed in F. I. Anderson, *Job*, Tyndale Old Testament Commentaries (Leicester: Inter-Varsity Press, 1976), pp. 41–55.

3. See Hebrews 12:3–11 which quotes Proverbs 3:11–12.

not mean that he was without sin, and therefore without need of correction. Nevertheless, the book makes it clear that Job's suffering is not directly connected with any sin on his part.

Those who say that the prose sections originally formed the story of Job, and that the poetry was inserted into it at a later date, have a point. The story alone makes quite good sense. Job is righteous and his faith is tested. His righteousness is proved as the test fails to move him from his trust in God. Thus he is vindicated and everything is restored to him. This kind of vindication is consistent with the stage of biblical revelation which preceded the revealing of life after death as the sphere of judgment and redress of wrongs. But the complete Book of Job is not interested in a doctrine which reduces the suffering of the righteous to testing of their faith. Nor does it suggest that suffering is something that we accept without questioning. We cannot suppose that the entire middle section of the book containing Job's search for understanding is put there so that it can be ruled out of order. Here is a piece of true wisdom in which the search for an understanding of God's ways refuses all trite answers which suggest either that we know it all or that we can know nothing.

Another way of stating the purpose of Job is that it is a striving for a theodicy. Theodicy means to justify the ways of God. In other words, the problem of the righteous sufferer seems to put God in a poor light. Someone will ask: 'How can God be a God of love if he lets such terrible things happen to innocent people?' Most of us will have worked out some kind of answer to this, and in so doing we have entered the realm of theodicy. In the New Testament one aspect of the answer lies in the future appearance of the kingdom of God and of his judgments.[4] This perspective of a future heavenly solution is not really open to the Old Testament. Furthermore, the future solution of the New Testament does not render the message of Job meaningless to Christians.

---

4. The suffering of Christians in relation to the coming kingdom is dealt with in my book *The Gospel in Revelation* (Exeter: Paternoster Press, 1984), ch. 2.

The variety of opinions about the purpose of Job indicates something of the complexity of its concern. Whether we see it as dealing with the righteous sufferer, with the meaning of faith, with the believer's sense of fellowship with God, or with the justification of the ways of a sovereign God, the book is still manifestly a wisdom book. To these other suggestions, all of which have something to contribute to our understanding of Job, we must add the overarching concern of the wisdom literature. Job is a book which asks, 'What is wisdom, and how can it be found?'

The crisis of wisdom

In the book of Proverbs we saw that the perception of order in the universe is a central concern of wisdom. Each observation based on experience invites us to try to understand it as fitting into a whole series of relationships with other events or experiences. Behind the order lies the creative activity of God, and the true understanding of all events must take account of God's revelation of himself. But even Proverbs recognizes that the orderliness of God's universe is sometimes very complex and hard to discern.

From the outset we can see that the arguments of the three friends of Job do not really apply to him. Their perception of order is very rigid and unable to handle exceptions to the 'normal'. We know Job is innocent. And Job, although he is unaware of God's approval as expressed in the prologue, nevertheless is sure that he has done nothing to merit such crushing misfortune. The friends argue the simple and, to them, obvious case that anyone who is on the receiving end of these calamities must indeed be a very great sinner.

Eliphaz is sure of his position because of a strange spiritual experience he claims to have had and which brought him out in goose-pimples (4:12–17). He poses the problem thus: either Job is unrighteous and deserves to suffer, or God is unrighteous for making him suffer. Since the latter is unthinkable, Job must be in the wrong:

> Can a mortal be more righteous than God?
> Can a man be more pure than his Maker?
>
> (Job 4:17)

Then comes Bildad whose appeal is not to spiritual experience but to tradition (8:8–10). He could have been a great teacher of wisdom if it were not for one thing. The truths he drew from the repository of past wisdom did not fit this particular case, and thus Bildad showed a fatal weakness in his understanding of wisdom. He had no better advice for Job than did Eliphaz, for he saw the solution only in Job's repentance:

> If you are pure and upright,
> even now he will rouse himself on your behalf
> and restore you to your rightful place.
>
> (Job 8:6)

Finally we have Zophar. He has been aptly described as a 'simple gospel' man.[5] It is all so clear, so black and white to this rigid and dogmatic man. He even suggests that God is being lenient with Job by overlooking some of his sins (11:6). Nevertheless he poses a real question that must be considered as part of the understanding of wisdom that the book is developing:

> Can you fathom the mysteries of God?
> Can you probe the limits of the Almighty?
>
> (Job 11:7)

Zophar clearly holds out little hope for Job's reformation and is quite scathing about it:

> But a witless man can no more become wise
> than a wild donkey's colt can be born a man.
>
> (Job 11:12)

Thus each in his own way rebukes Job for his sin and urges him to repent and so find favour once more with God. The

---

5. H. L. Ellison, *From Tragedy to Triumph* (Exeter: Paternoster Press, 1958), p. 49.

repetitions of this cycle of argument add little except more
and more heat to the discussion. Job, on the other hand,
continues to protest his innocence while paying little
attention to the friends' arguments. With great skill the poet
has our hero sparring with his opponents as if they were in
different rooms or on the opposite bank of a river. There is
never a head-on clash of ideas which leaves one or other the
clear winner. We may suggest that this clever arrangement
underlines the fact that the friends are never wholly wrong.
In this lies some of the appeal of the book. It is an exercise in
making contact between two aspects of wisdom. The one
stresses the observable patterns of cause and effect, while
the other stresses the mysteries of life's experiences.

So what does it mean to speak of the crisis of wisdom?[6]
The crisis occurred when a particular view of wisdom
hardened into a rigid interpretation of reality as a whole so
that it sometimes clashed with experience. It is fairly obvious
that Proverbs tends to emphasize the idea that there is a
close relationship between what we do and what happens as
a result. This is valid not only in the area of immediate cause
and effect, but also in the broader effects of ethical
behaviour. Many proverbs speak of the good that comes
from righteous or wise actions. This is not simply due to the
fact that the Old Testament has not arrived at a view of life
after death where all the scores can be settled. It really is a
fact of experience that good begets good and that wisdom
makes for life and its preservation. This deed-outcome
relationship is what we sometimes refer to as natural
retribution. We can observe it in our own experience so that
we are reassured that there is an order which prevails.

Natural retribution is something most people can understand. We know that there are laws of life which it is wise for
us to observe. There is little wisdom in living on a diet of
junk foods or in heavy smoking. On the broader level,
people are becoming more and more alarmed at the way we

---

6. This term is used by H. H. Schmid, *Wesen und Geschichte der
Weisheit* (Berlin: Alfred Töpelmann, 1966). See also H. D. Preuss,
'Erwägungen zum theologischer Ort alttestamentlicher Weisheitsliteratur',
Evangelische Theologie, Nr. 8. 1970.

are making our planet uninhabitable. The cultural mandate given to man by God has been distorted into the dogma of economic growth at any cost. The nuclear arms race and the threat of the extinction of all life on earth is the starkest reminder that we have of natural retribution. This kind of wisdom is characteristic of the book of Proverbs. But Proverbs does not try to reconcile the contradictions of experience, nor does it theorize about what lies behind them.

The crisis of wisdom is best illustrated in the book of Job. The three friends have a simple doctrine of retribution. But it is not as though they represent the wisdom of Proverbs in collision with Job's experience. Rather they represent the wisdom of Proverbs fossilized so that the time-relatedness of the proverbs is forgotten. It seems that they have made fixed general rules out of proverbial wisdom and are incapable of dealing with the apparent contradictions that experience throws up. Thus their arguments amount to this: many experiences show a direct relationship between righteousness and prosperity, between folly and evil; therefore all experiences of evil must be the direct result of unrighteousness.

The friends of Job are God-fearing men and it would be inconceivable that they had nothing at all to say that is valid. We may not dismiss them as irrelevant, for their words are essentially true. It is just that they do not apply to Job's situation. Job will appear as a challenge to Proverbs only if we follow the example of the friends and turn the proverbial statements into general rules. Job's experience was not new in Israel. The suffering of righteous people is to be found at all times, and the problem is summed up in the lamentation of the godly man oppressed by evil:

> How long, O Lord? Will you forget me for ever?
> How long will you hide your face from me?
>
> (Psalm 13:1)

Job's friends have not succeeded in handling the contradictions of their own proverbial style of wisdom. For example, the logic which they applied to Job could be extended to the poor of the world. There are a number of places in Proverbs which connect poverty with laziness or folly.[7] It would be easy to generalize this either by saying that laziness always begets poverty, or (worse) that poverty is always the result of laziness. The wise men clearly do not see it this way since they often show compassion for the poor and praise those that help them.[8] A poor man may even be the show piece of integrity (Proverbs 19:1).

The hiddenness of order

We may now return to the subject of faith and trust. It is recognized that the wise men of Israel were not humanists but, on the contrary, saw wisdom in the light of trust in God.[9] In our discussion of the fear of the Lord we saw something of the centrality to wisdom of faith in the God who is known by revelation. Many passages speak of trust in a way that goes beyond a response to the saving acts of God which are the pivot of Israel's covenant faith. In wisdom it is because the Lord has established order in the universe that our perception of this order in daily experience also invites trust in the Lord. The extraordinary claim of Proverbs 2: 1–15 is that the search for knowledge leads to an understanding of the fear of the Lord and to the knowledge of God. This underlines the point that the fear of the Lord is both our starting point and our goal. It is not that an objective examination of the universe by the open-minded unbeliever will lead him to acknowledge and trust God. Such a natural theology or perception of God is impossible. Rather it is the believer who accepts that God is the Creator, who then finds the whole universe reinforces this faith and trust.

Related to this idea of an orderly creation is the deed-outcome relationship of natural retribution. But what happens when experience contradicts this as in the case of Job? Wisdom had to come to terms with the fact that even wisdom as a gift of God did not imply that God teaches us to

---

7. Proverbs 6:6–11; 10:4,5; 12:11,24; 21:17,21,25.
8. Proverbs 14:21,31; 19:17; 21:13. This example from Hartmut Gese, *Lehre und Wirklichkeit in der alten Weisheit* (Tübingen: J. C. B. Mohr, 1958), p. 38.
9. G. von Rad, *Wisdom in Israel*, see especially Chapter 12.

think as he does with exhaustive or total knowledge of the universe. As von Rad puts it, some experiences put our trust under attack.[10] When this happens to us we may lose faith in the sense that we see the contradiction as removing all grounds for our previous trust. On the other hand, we could try a wiser path. We could take the contradiction as a reminder that we cannot see the whole picture. Only he who truly believes in the one creator God could accept this view. It is faith in the infinite, personal and caring God which distinguishes true wisdom from the intellectual conceit of humanism. The wise man is always aware that his search for knowledge is strictly limited by that infinite greatness which distinguishes God from man. In this he agrees with the prophetic word from God:

> As the heavens are higher than the earth,
> so are my ways higher than your ways
> and my thoughts than your thoughts.

(Isaiah 55:9)

Wisdom is aware of its limitations and it is ready to admit that there is much of God's order that is hidden from us. When faced with such mysteries it may be possible to see some reason in them. Wisdom acknowledges the function of suffering as training (Proverbs 3:11–12). But this is different from retribution only in degree, for correction implies some fault or imperfection that needs correction. This is certainly not the solution to the book of Job. The mystery is much deeper, and Job is left without even the assurance that a loving father is reproving him. His deepest suffering, surpassing that of his personal losses, is the silence of God.

Whatever we conclude about the originality of Job 28, this poem about wisdom is not irrelevant. From the frustrating failure of Job's friends to bring a solution to light we are taken to the heart of the problem:

> But where can wisdom be found?
> Where does understanding dwell?
> Man does not comprehend its worth;
> it cannot be found in the land of the living.

---

10. *Ibid.*

Where then does wisdom come from?
Where does understanding dwell?
It is hidden from the eyes of every living thing,
concealed even from the birds of the air.

God understands the way to it
and he alone knows where it dwells,
for he views the ends of the earth
and sees everything under the heavens.

(Job 28:12–13, 20–21, 23–24)

If God has created all things in order, then he alone has all wisdom. For man to pursue wisdom without this essential qualification is the height of folly. The human mind must accept that there is mystery which it cannot penetrate, an order which God maintains but which is hidden beyond our ability to find it. Even when wisdom is regenerated and linked with faith in the revealed word of the Lord, the wise man will view all the marvels of the creation which are before him and confess with Job:

And these are but the outer fringe of his works;
how faint the whisper we hear of him!
Who then can understand the thunder of his power?

(Job 26:14)

Before we consider God's answer to Job we should note one other theme. There is a deep consciousness in Job of the separation between man and God. That which Israel's religion depicted in so many vivid ways was forced upon him in an intensely personal manner. The ministry of the tabernacle with its fence and its veil before the most holy place, was a reminder that sin made a separation between man and God. The priest and all his blood sacrifices showed that only by a mediator could people approach God. What the prophetic word said to Israel was Job's deepest experience. He was cut off from God and he did not know how he could seek God's face again. Here it is not so much his sinfulness as his creatureliness which separates them. But the solution is the same; he needs a mediator:

> He is not a man like me that I might answer him,
> that we might confront each other in court.
> If only there were someone to arbitrate between us,
> to lay his hand upon us both,
> someone to remove God's rod from me,
> so that his terror would frighten me no more.
> Then I would speak up without fear of him,
> but as it now stands with me, I cannot.
>
> (Job 9:32–35)

Somewhere there must be such a one:

> Even now my witness is in heaven;
> my advocate is on high.
>
> (Job 16:19)

Then finally a passage which, despite its difficulty of translation from the Hebrew, expresses a confidence that death cannot mean a final separation from his God.

> I know that my Redeemer lives,
> and that in the end he will stand upon the earth.
> And after my skin has been destroyed,
> yet in my flesh I will see God.
>
> (Job 19:25–26)

This is not a full understanding of resurrection but rather a working through of what it means for God to be righteous. Undoubtedly it forms one part of the revelation which brings us towards the New Testament doctrine of resurrection. Its relationship to Job's desire for a mediator is important. Somehow his vindicator or redeemer will enable him to see God. He will not then need an explanation for to see God will be enough for him.

God's word on the matter

It is not until we are almost to the end of the book that for the first time God speaks to Job (38:1–41:34). The reply to Job's questionings is powerful, overwhelming, but not destructive. It is baffling in that it seems to avoid all the questions that Job and the friends have thrown up. The difficulty in pin-pointing the significance of this mighty oracle can be seen in the variety of scholarly conclusions that have been reached concerning it. Perhaps we can say two things about that: first, there is no answer to Job's questions and, second, to say there is no answer is to give an answer that is open ended in the way we perceive its applications. Another way of saying this is that God gives no direct answers to Job's questions about his suffering, but rather points to certain inevitable truths which lead Job on wisdom's path to a satisfactory conclusion of the matter.

God's words are not without rebuke:

> Who is this that darkens my counsel
> with words without knowledge?
>
> (Job 38:2)

Since in 42:7 God says that Job has spoken what is right about God, this verse cannot mean the opposite. Rather it indicates that Job is ignorant because he is without counsel on the matter.[11] So also:

> Will the one who contends with the Almighty correct him?
> Let him who accuses God answer him!
>
> (Job 40:2)

Job's answer (40:3–5) shows that the rebuke humbles him. But he has not yet reached the point to which God will bring him in the end. What, then, may we learn from this answer of God?

First, we may learn of God. The relentless questions put to Job confront him with the reality of the creation. This world in which Job lives is constant evidence of the order that embraces all things. The great poetic dialogues of the book show us the danger of thinking that by perceiving order in our limited experience, we thereby understand it all. It is a short step from seeing God as the creator and sustainer of order to thinking of God as himself bound to our simplistic

---

11. So Andersen, *Job*, p. 273f.

notions of order. When we begin to give independent status to things like order, justice, goodness and truth, it is not long before we also begin to insist that God should conform to them. We then build up a picture of a just and good God on the basis of the supposedly self-evident ideas of justice and goodness. The biblical picture is the opposite. God reveals what he is like and in so doing shows us what justice and goodness are. So with order; the revelation of God must define it for us. God is not a creature subject to a higher independent principle called order. Order is what it is because God is what he is, and because he made it so.

Job, then, learns of God as the God who is above the order which is perceptible to man.[12] This means that it is possible, indeed probable, that we all have experiences in which the deed-outcome relationship is really beyond our ability to perceive. The questions that God asks demand no answer, but rather invite Job once again to consider the greatness of the creation which bears witness to the kind of God that made it. What we sometimes refer to as the sovereignty of God, his absolute rule over all things, means that he is free. God is free, not to deny himself or capriciously to transform himself into a devil, but free nevertheless to do all things according to his will. That God reveals himself and makes himself knowable to us is a free act. The knowability of God must never be stretched so as to eliminate the mystery of God's unknowability. In other words, our knowledge of God is limited by what God chooses to reveal and by our ability to understand it. We must always allow that God is infinitely greater than our understanding can grasp both in his being and in his ways. Even the simple person can grasp that. On one occasion I asked a group of ghetto children in a New York childrens' shelter (where I worked as chaplain) what it would mean if we could understand everything about God. Without hesitation a diminutive seven-year-old showed wisdom beyond his years by answering, 'We'd be God!'

The silence of God had sat like an impenetrable mist on Job's world. While he was thus isolated from the one voice

---

12. Gese, *Lehre und Wirklichkeit*, p. 77.

that could give meaning to his experience, the arguments of the friends became to him as creature noises in his swamp of suffering. His misery, like a fog, blotted out all points of reference by which he could get his bearings and know himself in relation to some meaningful reality. The triumph of Job's faith lay in his perseverance of purpose to find meaning in God. Job's vindication lies in the fact that God speaks to him, not a word of final judgment, but a word which reconnects him with reality. God speaks with majesty, but it is the majesty that God was to reveal in Israel as a caring shepherd-like kingship.[13] God lovingly leads his son beyond the horizons of his own world of suffering. By God's word the healing is effected in a way that reveals God's wisdom as transcending the wisdom of men.

Learning wisdom from Job

Job's faith and trust penetrated the wall of silence more than he at first realized. He was as tenacious as a bull-dog in holding on to one thing: there must be an answer from God. Because his problem was wider than his suffering, Job speaks to those who suffer today and to a much wider audience. His problem lay in the fact that he lost the sense that anything had meaning. To compound the matter, God was silent. Everything that had made up his ordered existence was torn from him, but if God had only reassured him or told him of the arrangement with the satan things would have seemed different. Then there would have been suffering but not the same problem. It was as if all the living assurances that God, the shepherd of Israel, had given to his people were removed from Job's understanding. His was the suffering of a wordless pit that would bring him to understand the sufficiency of God's word to man.

The kind of suffering to which Job speaks is not only the literal horror of bereavement, destitution and social isolation

---

13. Compare with Isaiah 40:10–31. The Lord God who comes to rule Israel will feed his flock like a shepherd. It is remarkable that this description is followed by an oracle of creation which has much in common with the speech of God in Job.

that the story depicts. It speaks to our alienation from others and from the world. To the unbeliever who drowns his sense of meaninglessness and worthlessness in narcotic stupors, Job points to meaning as a gift from God to all who will trust him. His cry for a mediator reached out, in a way that he could not have understood, towards the Word of God who was to come in the flesh so that we, in our flesh, might see God.

For some the epilogue of Job is trivial and an anticlimax. Perhaps it does represent an editorial attempt that is less than perfect from a literary point of view. But from the point of view of the message of the book the epilogue confirms the significance of the oracle of God. Even though Job repents in dust and ashes we know this is not for the sin of which the friends accused him. Rather it means that Job has been lifted out of his desire for a straight answer from God. Lovingly God has brought him to see that the solution to his problem is not to become as God but rather to cast himself as the trusting creature upon the care of his Creator. The epilogue expresses in the only way possible for the people of the Old Testament the fact that Job was vindicated and restored to fellowship with God and man.

So Job does not contradict the wisdom of Proverbs. It goes beyond Proverbs by developing for us the meaning of the fear of the Lord and of the greatness of God. It reminds us that such fear of God is truly a reverent awe of one whose infinite greatness, wisdom and care reach far beyond anything we can comprehend. Job anticipates Paul's assurance that 'in all things God works for the good of those who love him, who have been called according to his purpose' (Romans 8:28). He reduces us to size so that we may be delivered from our conceit in thinking that our pursuit of wisdom will lead us to know all the answers. In Job's company we can be humbled by God only so that he might raise us up to a renewed trust in his goodness.

Questions for study

1. Summarize the structure of the book of Job by identifying its various parts.

2. Read Job 2–3 and in the light of these chapters describe

the emerging clash of wisdom ideas expressed by Eliphaz in Job 4.

3. What concept of order in the universe underlies the book of Job?

4. What do you consider to be the main lesson of Job?

8

Ecclesiastes and the Confusion of Order

Summary

Qohelet is a further expression of rebellion against a rigid form of Israelite wisdom. Again we are reminded that the search for order does not mean that everything is open to man's view. Thus there are times when certain approaches to wisdom seem to yield no results. This does not prove that there is no order, but only that it can be mysterious. Furthermore, human sin has confused both the order and our ability to know it. The wise response to the apparent darkness is to acknowledge the reality of God, to go on trusting him and to receive life as his gift.

The problem of Qohelet

The book of Proverbs, though cautious, is nevertheless optimistic in its view of the possibility for man to master the business of living as long as life is known to be the gift of God within an ordered universe. The book of Job makes a timely protest against the hardening of general patterns of retribution into a rigid dogma of cause and effect. Job warns us against the wrong interpretation of the wisdom of Proverbs which robs it of its relationship to time and history, that is, to the actual experiences of people. Another protest was raised against this generalizing of experience into strict rules, a protest which seems to lead its author to a position of hopelessness. 'All is vanity' says the preacher (or

Qohelet).[1] This refrain 'everything is meaningless' (NIV) occurs time and time again through the book and casts over it a mood of gloom and pessimism.

It is not difficult to understand why some critics have proposed that Ecclesiastes should be replaced by the more optimistic and more self-consciously Israelite wisdom of the book of Ecclesiasticus or, as it is also known, the Wisdom of Jesus ben Sirach.[2] However, the fact is that both Church and Synagogue accepted Qohelet and not ben Sirach as canonical Scripture. This presents us with the problem of how the theme of meaninglessness in Qohelet can be squared with the overall view of the Bible that a rational and personal God reveals himself and his purposes for his creation.[3]

Despite the difficulties in the apparent negativeness of the author, we have to say that he is no atheist and no stranger to the faith of Israel. Who was he? Tradition often identifies him as Solomon and it is sometimes suggested that this identification is the reason that the book was accepted into the canon of Scripture. Qohelet describes himself as the son of David (1:1), and also says that he *has* been king in Jerusalem (1:12). The omission of his name and the past tense (I was king) would both be inappropriate for a reigning monarch. As we shall see, the internal evidence of the book points to a later development in the wisdom tradition, and thus to a date later than Solomon. The term 'son of David' could refer to any descendant of David, but in this case it is probably a back-handed reference to Solomon, not to claim identity, but to indicate continuity with the wisdom traditions of Israel of which Solomon was regarded as being the fountain-head.

Apart from the recurring themes there is no obvious development in Qohelet. The apparent disconnectedness of the various literary units of the book has led many to suggest

---

1. *Qohelet* is the Hebrew word translated as preacher (RSV) or teacher (NIV). The root of the word signifies an assembly, the equivalent of the Greek *ekklesia*, and hence the name Ecclesiastes.

2. One of the wisdom books in the apocrypha.

3. The recurring Hebrew word is *hebel* which means vapour, vanity or that which has no substance. It is used over thirty times in Qohelet, sometimes in the intense form (vanity of vanities) and sometimes linked with a similar phrase 'a chasing after wind'.

that it is composite, embracing more than one point of view.
But in spite of the seeming randomness of the arrangement
of the material we find the constant theme inescapable: all is
meaningless. Ironically it is the placement of this theme which
rescues Qohelet from being for us a totally meaningless
book. It is not possible to confuse Qohelet's mood of
meaninglessness with the modern philosophy of nihilism.
Nihilism is the logical outworking of an atheistic view of the
universe. Once a personal and purposeful God is removed
from the scene, everything becomes the result of pure
chance and thus without meaning. Such a philosophy lies
behind the modern theatre of the absurd, Dadaism and
random composition music.[4] Atheistic nihilism is an impossible philosophy because it sets forth as meaningful the
proposition that nothing has meaning. Qohelet's cry of utter
meaninglessness is not of the same order. To begin with, he
is convinced of the reality of God and of meaning which is
known to God. That there is a personal, creator God makes
it possible for us mortals to grasp life as his gift, and that
alone gives reality meaning.

Of the various interpretations of this book there is one
that appeals more than most to evangelical Christians with
their high view of the inspiration of Scripture. It is proposed
that the author actually went through a period of searching
for the truth by means of various worldly ideas and pursuits,
or that he undertook a more objective investigation of these
godless approaches in order to test their validity. Either way
the result is the same. The secular approaches are shown to
be futile and only the fear of God is left as a viable
alternative.[5] On this view the contest in Qohelet is between
orthodoxy and worldliness, between faith in God and
practical atheism. Qohelet is an apologetic work, that is, an
argument for a particular view of reality which seeks to
establish its superiority over all other views. An interesting
variation on this general understanding of Qohelet is the

4. See James W. Sire, *The Universe Next Door*, pp. 76–97.
5. So G. S. Hendry, 'Ecclesiastes' in (ed.) F. Davidson, *The New Bible
Commentary* (London: Inter-Varsity Fellowship, 1953), also Derek
Kidner, *A Time to Mourn and a Time to Dance* (Leicester: Inter-Varsity
Press, 1976).

suggestion that it was written to oppose the evil influences of Solomon after his apostasy.[6] This supposes that Qohelet (Solomon) looks upon his own life as vanity and without meaning. The author of the book, having presented Solomon's view, rejects it and argues against it from the orthodox position of the fear of the Lord and the joy of serving him.

In my view these particular conservative positions do not really come to grips with the real nature of Qohelet. They appeal to us principally because they provide a fairly straightforward solution to the apparent contradictions and the difficulties of the book. We must beware of the tendency to rescue difficult parts of the Bible when they seem to strike a discordant note. What then are the other options open to us for an understanding of Qohelet? The view that it is a late work heavily influenced by Greek philosophy is not generally favoured by commentators any longer. Another approach is to see it as a notebook of the wise man's personal pilgrimage, thus accounting for the lack of form and the disarming honesty of the book. Others have suggested that the lack of form is explained if we suppose that it was originally a codex (a book with pages) rather than the usual scroll, and that the pages were put together in the wrong order. Still another view proposes that the book consists of an original composition of scepticism which was rescued for orthodoxy by the insertion of pieces of traditional wisdom. Most of these positions thus far mentioned have in common the idea that Qohelet is openly critical of some other approach to life. But to what does he really object? Is it to secularism, to Greek philosophical influences, to a scepticism that borders on atheism? If we can answer this we will be in a better position to understand the book as a whole.

The content and message of Qohelet

It would be difficult to show any developing theme running

---

6. Jack B. Scott, *God's Plan Unfolded*, revised edition (Wheaton: Tyndale House, 1978).

through the book, and the form of the finished work is part
of its problem. There is no question posed and answered.
However, there are some broad themes to be found. The
prevailing theme of meaninglessness is found throughout
from beginning (1:2) to end (12:8). Even in sections which
seem to depart momentarily from the prevailing gloom we
find this pessimistic word (2:26; 7:15; 8:10; 11:8; 12:8).
Nevertheless, Qohelet does stand in the wisdom tradition as
he asks questions about man's place in the total scheme of
things. Constantly he raises the matter of our portion or lot
(3:22; 5:18; 9:6,9), and our gain or benefit in life (e.g. 1:3;
2:11; 3:9; 5:16). Initially man's lot is seen as toil and vanity.
But is there no relief from this unpromising situation?

What is wisdom's answer? Qohelet appears to be against
wisdom at this point as he sets his mind to know how it can
help us (1:13, 16–18; 2:3,12). Wisdom, at best, is very
limited in its advantages (2:3,14; 4:13; 8:16–17). In fact
wisdom sometimes seems to be of no advantage at all, and
even to leave the wise man on an equal footing with the fool
(1:16–17; 2:14–17; 6:8; 9:11). Occasionally wisdom is given
some positive value (7:11–12,19; 8:1; 9:1; 13–18; 10:2,
10,12). This mixture of attitudes to wisdom is baffling on first
sight but if we bear in mind some of the characteristics of
wisdom itself we can make progress. Let us remember first
of all what we learned from Proverbs about the specific
nature of wisdom observations which allows contradictory
assertions to be placed side by side. At the level of day by
day experience there are many contradictions in life. Here
Qohelet does with the subject of the pursuit of wisdom what
Proverbs does with the general experiences of life. He
considers the gains of wisdom in concrete situations, not
from a general point of view or as a whole. Here wisdom
shows its positive gains, but there it is qualified, and there
again it seems to yield no advantage at all. Somehow the
search for order is confused and the wise man finds himself
standing with a feeling of nakedness and with nowhere to go.
God, it appears, has set wisdom within very strict limits
which prevent us from seeing a large enough picture of the
reality into which we must somehow fit.

In Proverbs we looked at the prevailing optimism of

wisdom in its perception of order in reality. Job was a revolt against the assumption that there are no mysteries in life. Now Qohelet looks at what appears to be a confusion of perceptible order. This confusion is more than the hiddenness to which the book of Job points. God is incomprehensible, but there is also the confusion injected by the human element of wickedness and oppression (3:16; 4:1–3; 5:8–9). This anticipates Paul's recognition that the creation has become subjected to futility because of sin and thus awaits its liberation along with the redeemed people of God (Romans 8:19–23).

Through all this comes the burning conviction of the unknowable nature of God. He is active in the world, but so much of what he does is unexplained and beyond finding out. Qohelet's scepticism is never in danger of becoming atheism for he knows that God is behind all this. Predestination is a fact of existence and everything has its appointed time (3:1–9), yet it is beyond our ability to penetrate it (3:10–11). There is nothing left for us to do but to live life a day at a time and fear God (3:12–15).

Despite his pessimism Qohelet can affirm life in God's world. It may not always be happy (1:13) but it is under God's control. Justice and judgment are real expressions of God's care (2:26; 3:17; 9:1; 11:9; 12:14). Thus, within the mystery and the confusion we can live knowing that life is God's gift and that there is some gain in being happy in our work (2:24; 3:10–15,22; 5:18–20; 9:7–10). Perhaps this is the most remarkable characteristic of Qohelet, that he refuses to give way to empty despair and so to say with the fool, 'There is no God'.

Learning wisdom from Qohelet

In questioning the traditional and conservative interpretation of Qohelet I would not say that it is totally wrong. Qohelet is not directly concerned with secularism, but indirectly he shows that it is not the answer to life's problems. He does this by affirming that the world is God's and that nothing happens by chance. But his main attack is directed at a form of Israelite wisdom that found a few simple answers to the question of our existence in the world. The friends of Job gave one expression of this dogmatic wisdom, which operated on a perceptible rule of retribution. This meant that the principal factor in world order is the immediate link of events to the deeds of men. The book of Job establishes the need for an intellectual revolt against such a view, yet without in any way conflicting with the wisdom of Proverbs. Qohelet goes further than Job in his revolt and shows the impossibility of a point of view which reduces God's action in the world to the wholly predictable.

It seems to be an unavoidable conclusion from both Job and Qohelet that Israelite wisdom had developed in a way that threatened its own validity. Perhaps it was the very perspective of wisdom which put it in jeopardy. By placing the history of Israel's salvation into the background, wisdom was always in danger of trying to construct a comprehensive view of the world of experience without reference to God's revealing acts. One consequence was the development of the dogmatic wisdom of Job's friends. Its attractiveness lay in its sense of perceptible order which was available to man. Its strict notions of retribution in life provided a firm basis for ethical judgement, and spoke of a justice in the universe which affected us at the level of daily existence. The warning for us here is that we should avoid the mistake of using proverbial wisdom as timeless general rules, as primarily ethical implications of the moral law of God.

The other development, due to wisdom's lack of specific concern for the history of God's saving acts in Israel, is a concentration on the fact of God as Creator. This is a perfectly valid perspective but carries with it certain dangers. The obvious pitfall is that the God-as-Creator notion may become virtually the whole of one's idea of God. God, when he is distanced from his saving acts, easily becomes an impersonal abstraction. The creation event is beyond our reach as an historical event, and we begin to think of God as some kind of non-personal force behind the universe.

In Qohelet the idea of a totally predictable God clashes with the reality of his mystery. This provides us with a creative tension which points us to towards a comprehensive wisdom which does not lose sight of God's revelation in history. In a sense the epilogue of the book shows that real life will always be lived in tension, at least in this world. Whether we see this as an orthodox postscript to Qohelet's sceptical clash with dogmatic wisdom, or whether we see it as Qohelet's own resolution of the conflict, the result is the same for us. We see the sage as a man of integrity who refuses to toe the line of the orthodoxy of his day for the sake of being known as doctrinally sound.

If we detect a note of despair in Qohelet, we should not write him off for his failure to be a victorious Christian. Great reformers are usually tormented men, and the road to reform is seldom easy. Those who would light a candle in the dark must first wrestle with the darkness and even risk being tainted by it before they can point the way through it. Qohelet is a rebuke to the false optimism which comes from a simplistic view of wisdom's goal. If he had managed to convey a sense of resolving the tensions he would have failed in his task. He sets God's sovereign will and purpose over against the apparent vanity of all things. But he will not give in to despair. He warns us against slick solutions of life's mysteries, so that we must always be open to having the lessons of our experience contradicted by further experience. He also warns us against something more subtle than blatant secular atheism, and that is trite religiosity.

It is futile to ask why Qohelet did not resolve the tensions by reference to the prophetic view of history and the future. It is wisdom's distinctive role to look at life more in terms of the present than of the past or future. It is thus that it avoids obscuring the tensions of human experience. We must affirm the soundness of the decision to recognise Qohelet as canonical Scripture rather than ben Sirach. The latter brought wisdom and the law of Moses together so that they were almost completely merged. This was no solution to any of the apparent problems of wisdom for in ben Sirach's time the law was fast being divorced from God's saving grace.

So we are rebuked by Qohelet for our tendency to take wisdom's remarkable sense of universal order and to turn it into a world-view which lacks depth, and which has no answer, other than condemnation, for the person whose experience contradicts it. From the New Testament perspective it is true to say that we can know with certainty that confusion and futility are banished by Christ. But until he comes again and all things are renewed, faith in the grace of God must sustain us through many incomprehensible tensions in our experience. The peculiar tension for the Christian is that we know our final goal with its resolution of all ills, but we do not know what tomorrow brings. Slick views on how to get guidance and to know God's will in daily things must go under the hammer of the crisis of wisdom in Job and Qohelet. This sceptical sage has an important lesson for us as he bids us take life a day at a time and enjoy it with its toil as a gift from God. He who truly fears God will stand in awe of the mystery of his ways among men.

Questions for study

1. What are the features of the book of Ecclesiastes which at first sight seem to contradict the prevailing view of God and man in the Old Testament?

2. What interpretations of Ecclesiastes have been proposed in order to account for its contents?

3. What are some of the wisdom themes found in this book?

4. What view of the order of the universe is found in Ecclesiastes?

9

Wisdom in all Manner of Places

Summary

Many attempts to identify wisdom influences in non-wisdom parts of the Old Testament seem to involve the assumption that the wisdom movement was quite separate from the rest of Israelite religious thought. There is no evidence for this. Rather we see wisdom and salvation history as two perspectives on the one reality. Both contributed to the Israelite understanding of reality. Nevertheless it is legitimate to try to identify the distinctive characteristics of wisdom and to look for possible wisdom influences in the mainstream of Old Testament salvation history and worship. The difficulty of doing this is increased by the resistance of the main wisdom writers to any extensive combination of wisdom and salvation history. The two converge and interact within two main areas of theology: in the doctrine of creation and in the royal theology of the wise king who rules within the context of God's saving acts.

The influence of the wise men

Since the wisdom literature contributes to our understanding of the world in which we live, it would be no surprise to discover that the wise men influenced the thinking of other Israelites. We have not found any evidence that they were rebels against Israelite religious thought or society. Were they, then, members of an identifiable group who were recognizable because they talked and wrote wisdom? Or were they less conspicuous members of the main-stream of

Israelite society? The few biblical references to individual
wise men and women, or to wise men as a recognizable
group, do not establish that the wisdom movement was a
clearly defined thing promoted by those who were known as
the wise men of Israel.[1]

If the men responsible for the wisdom literature of the
Bible were part of the community of the faithful it would be
strange if the distinctive ideas of wisdom did not show up
from time to time in other parts of the Old Testament. There
is good reason to believe that such influences do occur in
many writings of the prophets, in narratives and in a number
of psalms. It is harder to explain why the wise men
apparently resisted the influences in the opposite direction.
By avoiding almost all reference to prophetic faith, to
salvation history and law, the wisdom writers left us few
clues to how they saw themselves in relation to these
mainstream ideas of Israel's faith.

Unless we can stand close to the history of these things,
deciding what is an outside influence on someone and by
whom is not always easy. Fortunately we are able to observe
very clear characteristics of thought and language shared by
Proverbs, Job and Ecclesiastes. We can link these three
books as wisdom without suggesting a clearly defined
wisdom movement. We can observe also how these wisdom
books differ from the perspectives of the narrative and
prophetic writings. But if we are to suppose that significant
wisdom influences have occurred, we must be able to show
that it is the distinctly wisdom view of things that is
impressing itself upon the non-wisdom writing. This is easier
said than done. If wisdom was not a totally separate
movement, it is conceivable that some narrative historians
or prophets were also wise men. Then it would not be a
matter of influences at all, but rather one of different ways of
looking at things. It is important that we clearly understand
these different perspectives within the Old Testament and
their combined message for us.

The covenant theologians and the writers of salvation

---

1. e.g.: Exodus 36:4; Deuteronomy 1:13; 2 Samuel 14:2; Jeremiah
18:18; 50:35; 51:57.

history emphasized the nature of God's revelation through prophetic word and saving act. They recognized that God's word was the only true source of knowledge about the whole of reality. It would have been clear to them that God's word does not tell us everything about our existence, but it does provide us with the necessary framework within which we can seek to know life and the world about us. On the other hand, the wise men, assuming that which is revealed in God's word, set about the God-given task of understanding the complexities of human experience that are not directly the subject of revelation. If there were experts in both perspectives, we do not need to see that as presenting the ordinary Israelite with an either-or choice. Revelation, which leads to the fear of the Lord, has priority over human experience because without revelation sinful man is not able to discern ultimate truth from his experience. But at the same time we see that revelation tells us of our task of learning wisdom from experience.

Wisdom in non-wisdom books

Once it had been suggested that the wise men influenced non-wisdom writers, there followed a steady stream of scholarly proposals as to where the evidence for such influences may be found.[2] A few examples will do for the moment. It was claimed that the Joseph story in Genesis 37–50 showed all the signs of being a wisdom novel.[3] The reasons given are such things as advanced literary technique, enlightened cultural tone, and emphasis on human factors. The story is said to highlight wise counsel and administration, while Joseph overcomes adversity by prudence and the fear of the Lord. The arguments are rather less than convincing, although we have to agree that the story does contain themes and ideas that occur in the wisdom literature. Some

2. A useful survey is given by Donn F. Morgan, *Wisdom in the Old Testament Traditions* (Atlanta: John Knox Press, 1981).

3. G. von Rad, 'The Joseph Narrative and Ancient Wisdom', in *The Problem of the Hexateuch and Other Essays* (New York: McGraw Hill, 1966).

criteria given, such as interest in things outside of Israel's cult, are explicable by the fact that the events took place outside of Israel.

Another study places Amos the prophet in a wisdom context.[4] To be sure, Amos uses the numerical saying form that we observed in Proverbs (see Amos 1–2), but he does so in a manner which is different from that of Proverbs. Some have taken a more cautious approach and said that some prophets show that they were acquainted with wisdom and appreciated it.[5] Other parts of the Old Testament that have been nominated as showing the influence of wisdom include the books of Deuteronomy and Esther, the so-called succession narrative in 2 Samuel 9–20 and 1 Kings 1–2, and certain of the Psalms.

Most of the identifications of wisdom seem to assume that there were at least two distinct streams of thought in Israel which occasionally interacted. They highlight the problem of identifying wisdom as an entity, and of deciding what criteria can be used to identify its influences in non-wisdom literature. Many of the criteria proposed in these studies of alleged wisdom influences can be explained by the common background of history, experience and covenant faith.[6] It is, I believe, more satisfactory to refuse to segregate the wise men, and to see a plurality of perspectives dictated by the variety of concerns. What began with early folk wisdom in the home and market place would have developed within the overall perspective of the revealed faith of Israel. The interaction between the varous perspectives is found rather by looking for the emphases of the various books, both wisdom and non-wisdom, and by trying to understand the relationships between these different literary expressions. Here we are concerned with how the perspectives of Proverbs, Job and Ecclesiastes relate to the more prominent Old Testament themes of covenant and salvation.

---

4. H. W. Wolff, *Amos the Prophet* (Philadelphia: Fortress Press, 1973, German edition 1964).

5. J. Lindblom, 'Wisdom in the Old Testament Prophets', *Supplements to Vetus Testamentum*, III, 1955.

6. A stringent critique of many identifications of wisdom in non-wisdom books has been made by J. Crenshaw, *Journal of Biblical Literature*, 88, 1969, 129–142.

The wisdom psalms

A number of psalms are of special interest to us because they stand very close to the wisdom points of view. With a certain amount of confidence we can classify some of them as wisdom poems because they share the same distinctive emphases found in our major wisdom books. Other psalms invite our attention because they seem to join distinctively wisdom ideas with those of covenant and salvation history. There is a fair amount of scholarly agreement that the psalms which can be regarded as wisdom poems include Psalms 1, 37, 49, 73, 112, 127, 128 and 133, although there are some weighty protests against these opinions. Psalms 25, 34, 78, 111, 119 and 139 are considered to have been influenced to some degree by wisdom thought. Some psalms appear to place wisdom into a close relationship with the Israelite concept of salvation, and we may find them informative as to how the two perspectives interacted.

Psalm 78

The psalms illustrate in many places one of the basic principles of worship in Israel. Worship is ascribing worth to God which means responding to the way God has revealed himself to his people. The peculiar relationship of Israel to God focuses upon what God has done in saving his people. Thus all the words which describe God are given their definition in the acts of God as they are interpreted by his prophetic word. To worship God was, for Israel, to recall what God has done in the history of his saving acts.[7] It is this recital of salvation history that is not even hinted at in the main wisdom books.

Psalm 78 provides us with an unusual mixing of wisdom and salvation history. Although it is almost entirely given over to the events of Israel's past, it begins with a section that has a distinctly wisdom sound to it:

---

7. See Psalms 68, 98, 105, 106, 114 and 136 for examples of salvation history recitals. Many other psalms refer to the marvellous works of God or look at specific events which have saving significance.

O my people, hear my teaching;
listen to the words of my mouth.
I will open my mouth in parables,
I will utter things hidden from of old.

The call to hear, though not unique to wisdom, is suggestive of a teaching situation similar to that from which the instructions came. The word for *teaching* (Hebrew: *torah*) is also the word for God's law. Its root meaning is instruction and it always refers to God's instruction except here and in three wisdom passages (Proverbs 3:1; 4:2; 7:2) where it is the instruction given by a wisdom teacher. It is therefore probable that it is expressive of wisdom in this psalm.

The most significant wisdom indicators in Psalm 78 are the references to parables and hidden things in verse 2. The Hebrew word for parable is *mashal* which is used for proverb in the wisdom literature. This word has a diverse usage in the Old Testament but it appears to be rooted in popular wisdom. The hidden things translate the Hebrew *hidah* which is the word used for Samson's riddle (Judges 14), the queen of Sheba's hard questions (1 Kings 10) and Ezekiel's parable (Ezekiel 17). The overall impression of Psalm 78:1–3 is that of a wisdom teacher calling his pupils for instruction.

The problem of the psalm is that the instruction given is quite unlike any of the instructions given in the wisdom books. It is possible that it is a reworking of some older material which in this case consisted of a traditional salvation history recital. This is in keeping with verse 4:

We will not hide them from their children;
we will tell the next generation
the praiseworthy deeds of the Lord,
his power, and the wonders he has done.

But there are some significant differences from the usual salvation history recital.[8] The emphasis is more on the refusal of Israel to keep covenant with the Lord. The mighty

---

8. Other salvation history recitals are found in Exodus 15; Deuteronomy 26:5–9; Joshua 24; and Nehemiah 9.

deeds of God were intended to bind this people to himself, and so the word of God was given that they might not forget his saving acts (vv. 5–8). But Israel did not remember these things, either during the events or after. The miracle signs that God did in Egypt before the Exodus are seen as the prelude to Israel's disobedience in the wilderness. This faithlessness was the worse for being displayed in the midst of God's saving acts:

> In spite of this, they kept on sinning;
> in spite of his wonders, they did not believe. (v. 32)

> Their hearts were not loyal to him,
> they were not faithful to his covenant. (v. 37)

Once again the psalmist turns to the saving acts of God:

> They did not remember his power—
> the day he redeemed them from the oppressor,
> the day he displayed his miraculous signs in Egypt. (vv. 42–43)

Following this recital of salvation history (vv. 43–55) the theme of rebellion is again introduced (vv. 56–57), and this leads to the judgment on the temple in Shiloh (v. 60). Finally, God stirs himself to reject the northern tribe of Ephraim, and to establish his rule through David in Zion of the tribe of Judah. This latter section is unique to Psalm 78 out of all the salvation history recitals in the Old Testament.

This psalm takes the position of the book of Chronicles in emphasizing that God's purposes are removed from the northern tribes centred on Ephraim, and established in David. By recapitulating the miracles in Egypt the psalm links the great redemptive event in the Exodus with the climax of saving history in David's rule. We have noted already that David and Solomon are central to the development of the wisdom tradition in Israel, and that Solomon was remembered not only for wise rule, but also for the wisdom of ordinary human experience. Royal wisdom has its roots in this empirical wisdom, and it is by such wisdom that kings reign, as Proverbs 8:12–16 reminds us. It is not surprising that these ideals which were associated with

David and Solomon are taken up as characteristics of the messiah-prince of the house of David which the prophets expected. Observe the similarities in the relevant sections of Isaiah 11 and Proverbs 8 (RSV).

ISAIAH 11	PROVERBS 8
And the spirit of the Lord shall be upon him, the spirit of wisdom (*hokhmah*), and understanding (*binah*) . . . of counsel (*'etzah*) and might (*geburah*) . . . of knowledge and the fear of the Lord (v. 2) And his delight shall be in the fear of the Lord. (v. 3)	I, wisdom (*hokhmah*) . . . (v. 12) I have counsel (*'etzah*) and sound wisdom (*tushiah*) I have insight (*binah*) I have strength (*geburah*) (v. 14) The fear of the Lord is hatred of evil. (v. 13). By me kings reign. (v. 15)

This link between wisdom and the prophetic view of the messiah is relevant because the concluding section of Psalm 78 is suggestive of the messianic reign as the final outcome of God's redemptive acts:

> And David shepherded them with integrity of heart;
> with skilful hands he led them. (v. 72)

The final phrase is odd to say the least. But we note that the word translated *skilful* has a decidedly wisdom flavour.[9] The reference to his hand is a metaphor of David's kingly power.[10] The shepherd is also a commonly used image of rulership. In this context we may propose the translation of the last phrase as:

> And he guided them with the wisdom of his rule.

---

9. It is a noun in construct to *hands,* that is, it is the Hebrew way of saying *the skill of his hands.* The word *tebunah* is derived from the same root as *binah* noted above in Proverbs 8 and Isaiah 11. Of forty-one occurrences, five, possibly six, refer to a craftsman's skill, eight refer to God, and of these five concern creation (both are concerns of wisdom). Twenty-seven instances refer to human wisdom and twenty of these are in the wisdom books.

10. See Judges 6:13, 1 Samuel 4:3. The Hebrew *kaph* (palm of hand) is used with the same force as *yad* (hand) in 2 Samuel 8:3, Psalm 78:42 (NIV:power), Exodus 14:31.

What conclusions may we reach? We see in Psalm 78 a reshaping of the salvation history recital to make it the subject of a wisdom lesson. Here is the riddle of Israel's disobedience in the face of the astonishing grace of God shown in the redemption of Israel from Egypt in the Exodus. The solution to this problem of disobedience is found in the coming of the ideal rule of a kingship which is ordered according to true wisdom. The structure of the psalm emphasizes the rebellion of Israel against redeeming love. Then, by repeating the salvation history and extending it to David, it shows that the same events against which Israel rebelled are the solution to that rebellion. Salvation history is presented because it contains a riddle. It is joined to wisdom at the place where the two have long since met, in the royal wisdom.

Normally we would have expected salvation history to be outside the range of empirical wisdom. But something has happened in Psalm 78 to enable the totality of events from the Exodus to David's rule to be linked as one event to wisdom. The structure of the psalm is suggestive of a deliberate contrast of folly (Israel's rebellion) and wisdom (the wise rule of David). The events of salvation history, perhaps because of the passage of time, are able to be viewed by the psalmist as objective facts of Israel's experience. The retribution idea of Proverbs is at work: folly brings disaster, the wisdom of David saves the day and brings good. Thus, what would normally be a declaration of prophetic revelation is seen here through the eyes of the empirical observer. Even the pagans should have been able to see the wisdom of the nation through the effects of its covenant-keeping life. Instead, the stern warning of Deuteronomy has come true for a faithless nation:

> Observe them carefully, for this will show your wisdom and understanding to the nations, who will hear about all these decrees and say, 'Surely this great nation is a wise and understanding people.'
>
> (Deuteronomy 4:6)

However, if you do not obey the Lord your God . . . You

will become a thing of horror and an object of scorn
(Hebrew: *mashal*=proverb) and ridicule to all the nations.
                                        (Deuteronomy 28:15,37)

But then wisdom triumphs in the glorious reign of David.
The divinely placed order of the universe is established as
the order of Israel's existence under the ideal messiah-king.
He is the good shepherd whose royal wisdom restores his
people.

Psalm 73

This psalm is also widely accepted as a wisdom poem,
although it is not clearly grounded in the older folk wisdom
of Israel. It can be regarded as a didactic composition, that
is, one that is intended to instruct others. It raises the matter
of theodicy which, though dealt with in wisdom, is by no
means unique to it. The specific form of the problem is the
arrogance of the prosperous evildoers who interpret their
ability to gain through their unrighteousness as a proof that
God is without knowledge (v. 11). The psalmist feels that his
own righteousness has been in vain for he has no benefit
from it.

In a sense this psalm ploughs the same ground as Job and
Qohelet. But its answer is wholly different, and herein lies
its special interest for us. The deed-outcome relationship, so
prominent in Proverbs, is under attack. The evil man
prospers and the good man suffers adversity. The solution is
that the psalmist enters the sanctuary and comes near to
God. We must not forget how important the actual place of
the temple was for the Israelite even though he knew that
God was not confined to the temple precincts. It was
through the services and sacrifices held in that special place
that the faithful drew near to God.

The significance of Psalm 73 is that it is a wisdom poem
written from within the context of the temple cult. It thus
provides us with a rare glimpse of how wisdom may have
been merged with the prophetic faith of Israel. There are at
least two possibilities here. The first is that wisdom is being
adapted to the framework of Israel's law and temple
worship. What God has done in his saving acts in history is

given as the basis of confidence in the face of the apparent attack on the order of things. The second is that the wisdom perspective with its very individualistic standpoint is brought to bear on the ritual practices of the cult in order to focus on the inward reality to which the cult points, but which has always been in danger of mere outward observance.[11] It is the circumcision of the heart (Deuteronomy 30:6) rather than outward ritual that was needed.

This drawing together of wisdom and temple worship is no surprise. What is perhaps surprising, given the relationship of Solomon the temple builder to wisdom, is that there was not much more exploration of this relationship in the wisdom writings and elsewhere. It seems that most of the wisdom writers were content to presuppose the fear of the Lord, a concept born out of salvation history. Wisdom comes from God, and the wisdom of God is expressed in his revealed truth including the specific details of law given to Israel. While most of the wisdom writers pursued the matters of personal experience and of our humanity within this world, occasionally the question of Israel's covenant faith intruded into distinctly wisdom concerns.

Torah and wisdom

If the fear of the Lord means, among other things, covenant faithfulness and observance of the law (torah), what connection was the law seen to have with wisdom? Many scholars have considered the apparent wisdom influences in the book of Deuteronomy.[12] Deuteronomy brings a concern for salvation history and the law into view with a number of themes and emphases that are shared with the wisdom books. But how far this means that wisdom influences are at work is difficult to say. One writer suggests the following

11. Hans-Jürgen Hermisson, *Sprache und Ritus im alttestamentlichen Kult* (Neukirchen-Vluyn: Neukirchener Verlag, 1965), p. 146f.

12. E.g.: M. Weinfeld, 'Deuteronomy—the present state of the enquiry', *Journal of Biblical Literature*, LXXXVI (1967), 249–262, and Joseph Blenkinsop, *Wisdom and Law in the Old Testament* (New York: Oxford University Press, 1983).

wisdom traits in Deuteronomy: the idea of direct retribution coupled with the theme of 'life', education of children, and the spiritualizing of the faith away from mere ritual observance.[13] These catagories are too broad in that they are found also in areas where no wisdom distinctives are present. They can be no more than merely suggestive of wisdom influences here.

As a body of literature the Apocrypha is important to us in that it reveals a great deal about the religious and literary developments that took place between the Old and New Testaments. There are some significant wisdom works in this literature which were never included in the canon of Scripture. The most important is the Wisdom of Jesus ben Sirach, or Ecclesiasticus (not to be confused with the biblical Ecclesiastes). It was written by a wise man of Jerusalem in the early second century BC. Its main interest for us is its clear dependence on the traditions of Solomonic wisdom and its inclusion of law and salvation history. The style of ben Sirach is much more reflective than Proverbs, and it seems that he was facing the question of how the wisdom and salvation history perspectives may be drawn together. As in Proverbs wisdom is the achievement of men as well as a gift of God who is its source. Ben Sirach points to the law as a principal way in which the wisdom of God comes to reside in Israel: (here wisdom is speaking)

> Then the Creator of the universe laid a command upon me;
> my Creator decreed where I should dwell.
> He said, 'Make your home in Jacob;
> find your heritage in Israel.'
> Before time began he created me,
> and I shall remain forever.
> In the sacred tent I ministered in his presence,
> and so I came to be established in Zion.
>
> (Ecclesiasticus 24:8–10, NEB)

The last part of ben Sirach is a kind of salvation history recital from beginning to end. But it is not the usual

---

13. Weinfeld, *op. cit.*

recounting of the mighty acts of God. Rather the emphasis is on the people involved and their virtues:

> Let us now sing the praises of famous men,
> the heroes of our nation's history,
> through whom the Lord established his renown,
> and revealed his majesty in each succeeding age.
>   (Ecclesiasticus 44:1–2, NEB)

Ben Sirach does not include wisdom under law, but rather turns law and salvation history to become expressions of the wisdom of God among his people Israel.[14] He presents a particular development of Old Testament perspectives on the wisdom of God. This tendency towards a full identification of wisdom and law ignores the fact that wisdom functioned as a loosening of the absolute tutelage of the law. The direction that ben Sirach takes would, I suggest, lead us towards something other than fulfilment in the gospel. The disqualification of this book from the canon of Scripture is soundly based.

Conclusion

The question of wisdom influences in non-wisdom books must remain open. At best, it seems we can detect the merging of certain perspectives which are characteristic of wisdom on the one hand and of salvation history on the other. There is no good reason for separating the origins of these strands into totally unrelated areas. We have noted that wisdom from human experience is characteristic of every culture, it is a part of being human. Likewise, every culture wrestles with the relationship of experience to the religious ideas which are held, particularly insofar as these ideas are thought of as having a distinct source in an authoritative revelation.

Because Israel's prophetic faith resisted all tendencies to pantheism which blurs the distinction between God, man and the world, the relation of human thought and action to

---

14. So von Rad, *Wisdom in Israel*, chapter 13.

the divine thought and action always retained an element of mystery. Wisdom acknowledged that the wisdom of God was somehow there behind all true wisdom in men. It did not try to analyse this relationship but placed the two elements side by side. The specific form of the problem for wisdom is how the task of the human quest for knowledge relates to the gift of the grace of God in saving act and revelation. Since wisdom is concerned with the whole created order, and since Israel's salvation history was never divorced from this created order, it is only to be expected that the relationship of salvation history to created order would in time force the wisdom and covenant perspectives into converging paths.[15] Wisdom and law both point to human responsibility before the one God whose wisdom is the source of both. It would be strange if wisdom did not find itself included in the perspectives of law and prophecy.

These tensions in Old Testament thought must be set with all other aspects of Old Testament thought which raise the question of what it means to be human in God's world. Only in the place where God and man most perfectly relate will we find the last word on the matter. Here we will discover that to be human is not to solve the mystery nor to resolve the tension. The wisdom of God will be found to be the perfect union in the God-man Jesus Christ. Insofar as he preserves the mystery by being both God and man, he reminds us that somehow human wisdom is gift and task. It always remains distinct, though not separate, from its source—the wisdom of God.

Questions for study
1. Suggest some of the characteristics of form or thought which might indicate wisdom influences in material which would not be regarded as wisdom literature.
2. On what grounds could it be argued that Psalms 1, 37 and 111 are either wisdom poems or are influenced by wisdom?
3. What contacts between wisdom and salvation history do we find in the Old Testament?

---

15. Donn F. Morgan, *op. cit.*, p. 53.

10

Wisdom in Old Testament Theology

Summary

The theology of wisdom makes contact with covenant theology in a number of ways. The God of the covenant was perceived to be the God of all creation and human existence. The wise men operated within the covenant as they explored God's creation. Creation itself implied the covenant. It spoke not only of what was once perfect but is now imperfect because of sin, but also of what will again be perfected through redemption. Wisdom explored a concept of righteousness that embraced the whole world order. Wisdom is not natural revelation but a way of interpreting nature and experience within the reality that is revealed in God's word. Thus wisdom has no independent theology. It depends upon, and is closely integrated with, the progressive revelation of God's kingdom. There is a special point at which wisdom theology converges on covenant in the wisdom of Solomon and in the subsequent prophetic idea of the wise messianic prince. This points finally to the New Testament perspective on Christ as the fulfilment of all the Old Testament expectations, including those of the perfecting of wisdom.

Wisdom and the kingdom of God

It is now time to try to draw together some of the threads. Elsewhere I have proposed that one way of looking at the overall message of salvation is as the re-establishment of

God's kingdom.[1] We can reduce the New Testament idea of the kingdom of God to some basic elements which are recognizable throughout the whole biblical story from creation to new creation. They are: God, mankind and the created universe all relating in the way God intended. Not only are these the essential ingredients of what the Bible is on about, they also include everything that exists. Thus we can say that reality (everything that exists) is God, man and creation. The kingdom of God is God, man and creation properly related to one another. What we have referred to as salvation history involves the whole process within history by which God saves, which means that he renews the relationships which were dislocated through human sin. But wisdom gives us another perspective on God, man and creation. The problem is how this perspective relates to that of salvation history.[2]

All religions and philosophies deal with the relationships between God (or gods), man and the world, even if they begin by asserting, or assuming that there is no God. So we haven't really got very far by saying that both wisdom and salvation history in the Old Testament are concerned about these three aspects of reality. But do their respective views or perspectives actually make contact? So far we have seen that there are many reasons for saying that they do. In looking at the history of wisdom in Israel and at the main wisdom books, we have seen many points of contact and overlap with the larger body of Old Testament literature dealing with the saving acts of God and their accompanying elements of covenant, law, cultic worship and prophecy.

Worldly wisdom or wisdom of the world?

There was a time when wisdom sayings which contained no

---

1. See my book *Gospel and Kingdom*.
2. I have made some preliminary study of this relationship at a theoretical level in: 'The problem of the accommodation of wisdom literature in the writing of Old Testament theologies', (unpublished Th.M. dissertation, Union Theological Seminary in Virginia, 1970). I have also investigated a specific area of the problem in: 'Empirical wisdom in relation to salvation history in the Psalms', (unpublished Th.D. thesis, Union Theological Seminary in Virginia, 1973).

reference to God, or no explicit concern with Israel's covenant thinking, were regarded as non-theological or secular. We now recognize the inadequacy of this judgment. And in this regard we should not misunderstand Paul's contrast between worldly wisdom and true wisdom. True wisdom includes a way of looking at the world. It is worldly in the proper sense of providing the basis for life in the world. It should not be confused with an atheistic world view because it proceeds from the fact of God as both Creator and Redeemer of the world.

The biblical wisdom that is without 'God-talk' is now recognised as being empirical in the sense of being based on human experience. But it does not fit the evidence to say that there is no thought of God behind it. The problem has been to understand precisely in what way empirical wisdom relates to the knowledge of God and man which is revealed in the inspired prophetic word. Even if those responsible for the propagation of folk wisdom and empirical wisdom in general never thought about this relationship, there came a time when both strands were seen to be expressions of a unified truth. We must take seriously the canonization of Scripture which was the recognition of the whole of it as God's word to his people.

Thus, what may at first seem to be a placing side by side of two quite irreconcilable views of reality, may in fact be the meeting of two different but valid perspectives of the same reality. The empirical wisdom of the Old Testament is not a godless or pagan assessment of reality. It is the work of Israelites who, precisely because of their heritage in the covenant and the history of God's saving acts, are driven to find a unitary view of the world. The implications of the salvation of Noah, of the covenant with Abraham, of the Exodus from Egypt, of Sinai and the theocratic state of Israel, are that the Lord God of Israel reigns in heaven above and in the earth beneath. Furthermore, the Israelites, though plagued by many forms of idolatry that came beating at their door, were as yet unaffected by the Greek thinking which rejected the world and everything material. If God was saving Israel it was into an earthly kingdom in the land of Canaan. Some people despise the apparently crude

materialism of the Old Testament view of the kingdom of
God, and flee to what they think are purer notions of spirit
and the immortality of the soul. On both counts they betray
a paganism as bad as anything that the Israelites toyed with.
Spirituality in the Old Testament was never a world-hating
retreat from materialism. Rather it was established on the
covenant of God to man which restored man to right
relationships with God and with the created order. It is
ironic that the worldly wisdom which Paul shuns in 1 Corinthians is one which adopts a phoney spirituality without the
world of matter, while true spirituality involves a wisdom
that learns to understand the world in relation to God.

Wisdom and creation

The broad study of wisdom seems to show two things. First,
the wisdom writers were Israelites through and through, and
they acknowledged the prophetically revealed word of God.
They did not reject the covenant but rather operated within
this framework of the fear of the Lord. Secondly, despite
this orthodox Israelite mind-set, the wisdom writers found
that their subject matter and method of approach did not
involve them in specific concerns of the covenant and the
saving acts of God. Rather they looked at man in the world
at large. Because of this, it has been suggested that wisdom
is a working through of a theology of creation. If this is an
accurate assessment, a warning must be sounded. Creation
and salvation do not involve two totally different world-
views in the Old Testament. Indeed, Israel's view of creation
cannot really be understood apart from the doctrines of
redemption. Nevertheless, we can concentrate our attention
on one or the other without ignoring their close relationship.

A modern example may help us to see the issues which
faced the wise men of Israel. In our twentieth-century
western culture we can see at least two models of comprehensive Christian education in day schools. A more traditional
model emerged when church and state were much more
closely aligned than they are today. The curriculum mirrored
the view of reality held by a society which was largely

thought of as Christian. With the gradual secularizing of society and the breakdown of Christian values, the educational curriculum of many institutions simply followed the same process of secularization. A school chaplain and weekly religious instruction were all that marked the school out as Christian. The chaplain did his bit according to his convictions to try to inject a bit of Christianity into the pupils' thinking. Meanwhile, a largely secular staff taught subjects from the same humanist perspectives as those which came to be established in state run schools. The traditional church-linked schools of today frequently exhibit this pattern. Such schools are often Christian in name only and in their being to some degree controlled by denominational synods or assemblies. There is no overall Christian view of reality underpinning their educational processes.

A relatively new phenomenon is the independent Christian school often organized on the 'parent-controlled' principle. This is a deliberate move by Christians to break the stranglehold on education of a secular humanist state.[3] Two distinct issues are involved. One is the right of Christian parents to control the education of their children. The other is the importance of a distinctly Christian view of reality. Some Christian schools have successfully established a measure of parental control within the limits of a state imposed standard, but find the development of a curriculum which embraces the whole of education within a Christian framework a much more difficult matter. Christian educators are being forced to ask whether being Christian affects in any marked way the approach we should adopt to teaching science, language, the humanities and mathematics. It is recognized that making Bible knowledge a full compulsory subject, teaching creation as an alternative model of origins to evolution, and using the Bible as a reading text, does not necessarily make the curriculum Christian. But what, after all, is a Christian approach to mathematics, or to the study of Japanese or Indonesian? The task is not so much to make these subjects somehow religious in themselves, as to find

3. R. J. Rushdoony, *Intellectual Schizophrenia* (Phillipsburg: Presbyterian and Reformed Publishing Company, 1978).

their relationship to an integrated Christian interpretation of the world and of our place in it. I suggest that the wisdom literature of the Bible has something to teach us here.

In order to understand the relationship of wisdom to a theology of creation we need to look at the possibilities of such a theology. Creation may be taken into account with an accent on origins. In the ongoing debate about creation and evolution, creation may be proposed as an alternative explanation of origins. Proponents of special creation point to the philosophical and scientific inadequacies of evolutionary dogma in its attempt to explain how we came to be here. It is doubtful, however, that the biblical doctrine of creation arose primarily out of a concern about origins. Without entirely discarding the question of origins, we may propose that the biblical view of creation has its emphasis on relationships. Of course origins and relationships are inseparable, but we need to understand the perspective in which they come to us in the Bible. To do that we will have to go back behind the creation-evolution debate to something more basic: how do God, man and the universe relate? In a real sense the doctrine of creation is an implication of what the Bible says about God's character as a just and redeeming God.[4]

The place of creation in Old Testament theology is open to debate. There is little doubt, however, that the Old Testament writers saw creation more for its present implications than for its solution to the question of how we began. In this they are in full accord with Paul's extraordinary statement in Colossians 1:15–20 where creation's blueprint is the person and saving work of Christ. If Paul sees the gospel here as God's forethought to creation, the Old Testament prophets and historians see creation as the prelude to salvation history. Indeed, the whole biblical understanding of regeneration (re-creation) as the kernel of salvation, stems from the Old Testament view of creation and re-creation. In all this the matter of relationships is central. Genesis 1–2 stress the personal element in that the infinite,

---

4. J. L. Crenshaw, *Studies in Ancient Israelite Wisdom Literature* (New York: *KTAV, 1976), pp. 1–45.*

personal Creator brings things to be by the most distinctly inter-personal trait: the spoken word. If the Israelite asked the question, 'Where did I come from?' there is no doubt that the answer would be creation. But the prophetic view of redemption—a restoration and a buying back—implies that the constant emphasis on the new world order to come is a re-establishing of the original world order. Both old and new creations are the work of the one Creator. The emphasis is far more on where we are now and where we are going, than on where we came from.

Thus, without denying the question of origins, we see creation in the Old Testament as a way of giving meaning to the present and the future. If we are in need of redemption then we have fallen. If we have fallen then we have fallen from something. That something was a realm of relationships ordered by God, and that can be only if God is the one who created all things freely and sovereignly. We can understand, then, why some Old Testament scholars maintain that the real heart of the Old Testament is not salvation history but the creation of an orderly universe.[5] Creation becomes for us the rule of order. The prophetic view of the future, that order is being restored through redemption, reminds us that order still exists, though it is obscured to some degree by the forces of chaos.

Righteousness

Creation also provides a basis for understanding the biblical terms *righteousness* and *justice*. These two words are prominent in the Old Testament, especially in the prophets. They are constantly linked with God's judging and saving roles. Because they are usually connected with legal and moral ideas in the non-religious realm, we tend to think of

5. J. L. Crenshaw, *Studies in Ancient Israelite Wisdom Literature*, pp. 26–35. H. H. Schmid, '*Schöpfung, Gerechtigkeit und Heil*' in *Altorientalische Welt in der alttestamentlichen Theologie* (Zurich: Theologischer Verlag Zurich, 1974). Hans-Jürgen Hermisson, 'Observations on the creation theology in wisdom' in (ed.) J. Gammie, *Israelite Wisdom* (Missoula: Scholars Press, 1978).

their biblical use as likewise legal and moral. Such an assumption is being seriously questioned on the basis of the biblical evidence. One leading scholar, having examined the usage of righteousness in the Old Testament, argues that its meaning has to do with the created order in the universe.[6] This means that righteousness, while including human responsibility, embraces the whole of creation. Legal and moral ideas are derivative of this.

The creation-related idea of righteousness points to the harmonious principle underlying the order established by God at creation, and which is an aspect of the character of God imprinted on the creation. The restoration of the creation, as an integral part of salvation, is a restoration of justice and righteousness.[7] So Isaiah looks forward to the time when:

> . . . the Spirit is poured upon us from on high,
> and the desert becomes a fertile field,
> and the fertile field seems like a forest.
> Justice will dwell in the desert
> and righteousness live in the fertile field.
> The fruit of righteousness will be peace;
> the effect of righteousness will be quietness
> and confidence forever.
> My people will live in peaceful dwelling-places,
> in secure homes,
> in undisturbed places of rest.   (Isaiah 32:15–18)

Here justice and righteousness mean that nature and man are restored to harmony as a result of the saving acts of God. Thus, while it is impossible to fit all the uses of righteousness into a legal-moral framework, it is possible to fit them, including the legal-moral, into a framework of universal order.

While the wisdom literature is lacking in the salvation

---

6. H. H. Schmid, *Gerechtigkeit als Weltordnung* (Tübingen: J. C. B. Mohr, 1968). Schmid maintains that we can see six distinct areas in which righteousness is used: juristic, wisdom, nature, salvation, cult and sacrifice, kingship.

7. Justice (Hebrew, *mishpat*) and righteousness (Hebrew, *tzedeq*) are frequently linked and may be regarded as virtually synonymous terms.

perspectives, it uses the word righteousness frequently. It is likely, in the light of the considerations of order that we have observed in the wisdom books, that we have here an emphasis on the wider concept of righteousness as universal order. More recent studies have reminded us that it used to be accepted that wisdom was utilitarian and eudaemonistic in outlook.[8] Utilitarianism is a view of life that assesses things and actions by their usefulness. Eudaemonism assesses them according to the happiness they produce. Such a view of wisdom is no longer held. Rather, as H. H. Schmid suggests, the chief question of Israel's wisdom thinking is: how does one recognize the order of the world which is established and guaranteed by God?[9]

To this end, the prologue of Proverbs indicates that the purpose of wisdom is instruction in righteousness (*tzedeq*), justice (*mishpat*) and equity (Proverbs 1:3). References to righteousness and the righteous person abound in the proverbial sentences. In most cases there is a contrast between the righteous and the wicked which reminds us that the moral sense is there. But it is wider than that. The contrasts of righteous and wicked are constantly posed in terms of the successful life of the former and the confusion of the latter. The religious context of covenant (the fear of the Lord), among other things, demanded that the perceptible relationships between one's manner of life and its outcome be assessed more accurately than as an expression of eudaemonism. The challenges to the perceptible order posed by Job and Ecclesiastes, do not in any way rule out the deed-outcome relationship of Proverbs. The proverbial literature is saying that despite the exceptions and the mysteries, there is a discernible relationship between life-style and outcome. The principle of order includes everything that God has specifically revealed in his law, and thus includes the legal-ethical idea of righteousness. But it goes beyond this to embrace the whole range of human existence in the world. The fact that God is the Creator of the world means that even those areas of human action which appear

---

8. H. H. Schmid, *Gerchtigkeit als Weltordnung*, pp. 96–98.
9. *Ibid.*

to be ethically neutral or which do not come within the scope of the revealed law of God or of the law of society, are within the scope of righteousness. In so saying, wisdom points to the truth that there are no neutral actions, no neutral thoughts.

Revelation

A consideration which follows from the nature of wisdom is that of natural revelation and natural law. If the scope of wisdom is beyond that of the specific word-revelation of God, does that mean that there is truth to be discerned from the world quite apart from God's prophetic revelation? Natural revelation means that truth about God is imprinted upon the creation. Natural theology assumes that this truth can be discerned from nature by means of our human senses without the aid of Scripture or the Holy Spirit. Natural law refers to a specific aspect of natural theology, namely, that part of such discernible revelation is a range of self-evident ethical principles. There are significant theological disagreements over this question. But we must consider the matter because it might appear to some that the implication of what we are saying is that there are two distinct sources of ultimate truth: revelation through God's word, and observation of experience in the world. Human behaviour would then be governed by God's words and by discernible rules of nature. Knowledge of God would come to us by the word of God and by our observation of the universe which bears the stamp of God's character.

We must first dispense with the idea that wisdom is Israelite humanism in the sense that man is the centre of things and is capable of interpreting the universe on his own. Wisdom is truly humanitarian in its concern for people and their well-being, but it is not humanistic. Humanism as a philosophical system rejects the possibility of God as the ultimate reality. If there is a God he is subject to the same laws of being as the rest of the universe. This is not the God of the Bible. Wisdom, even in its most sceptical moments (Ecclesiastes), never contemplated anything but a universe which is creature, and therefore subject to the laws of a personal, eternal and sovereign Creator.

Next, we must rule out the idea that real truth is discernible from both revelation and nature independently. Order was perceived by ancient religions and pagan wisdom, and it goes on being perceived in modern philosophy and experimental science. But it was, and is, a warped perception because it does not start from the facts given by revelation of an eternal, personal God who is the ultimate source of all things and their order. But there are Christians who adopt the position that creation is able to reveal to us truth about the existence of God the Creator, and thus natural theology is possible.[10] This means that without considering the truths that come only by special revelation, we can understand truly, even if only partially, the meaning of the universe. It is claimed that Romans 1:20–32 establishes this position. But what Paul in fact says is that God has revealed himself in creation, but that it is the nature of human sin to repress that revelation. Men knew God through the creation but did not acknowledge him. Rather, 'their thinking became futile and their foolish hearts were darkened' (v. 21). 'They exchanged the truth of God for a lie, and worshipped and served created things rather than the Creator' (v. 25). 'Since they did not think it worth while to retain the knowledge of God, he gave them over to a depraved mind, to do what ought not to be done' (v. 28). The problem with natural theology is that it does not recognize the naked rebellion of sin with the depravity of mind that it produces.

Wisdom is clearly not engaged in natural theology. It does not assume any neutral ground of knowledge open to all men alike. Its indisputable presupposition is God the Creator. But from where did this starting point come? The

---

10. Thomas Aquinas (died 1274) proposed that revelation came through nature plus grace (special revelation). His thought was the basis of the position known as Scholasticism. This maintained that man is capable of establishing a valid natural philosophy, that is, a concept of truth through nature apart from the special revelation of the Bible as it is applied to us by the Holy Spirit. This has far reaching consequences for the interpretation of the Bible, for the self-evident truths of natural philosophy are adopted as the framework within which special revelation is understood and interpreted.

answer is special revelation. Israel's prophetic revelation of YHVH (or Jehovah) making covenant and acting to save his people undergirds true wisdom. It is the fear of the Lord which enabled the wise men to know what is the meaning of all life's experiences. Without a knowledge of the God of salvation history, there could be no true wisdom, no real knowledge of the world.

The contacts between Israel's wisdom and that of Egypt or Mesopotamia may suggest real common ground. But this is a superficial assessment. It was not that they all truly knew something of the ultimate meaning of the universe, and that Israel's wisdom was given a special boost by the addition of revealed knowledge. If the fear of the Lord is the beginning of wisdom, it can in no sense be merely a supplementary boost to common wisdom. Israel's wisdom says that only through the fear of the Lord can we know anything truly. Wisdom can never give ultimate meaning to the world of our experience except in terms of the Lord's creative and saving acts. Whenever Israel's wisdom seemed to coincide with Egypt's, or Solomon's with the queen of Sheba's, it was because they were operating at the level of immediate meaning, not ultimate meaning. An Israelite and an Egyptian might learn and state similar things from similar experiences. But the Israelite would explain the reality in the light of the revelation of the creator God of Israel as he reveals himself by his word. The Egyptian, on the other hand, would appeal to Ma'at, a no-god conceived in the minds of sinful men who have exchanged the truth of God for a lie. It is not possible rightly to interpret reality on the basis of a lie. Modern atheistic humanism sees ultimate meaning from the perspective of man as the final interpreter. In its relation to modern thought, Israel's wisdom shows a very contemporary concern for all life in this world, but refuses to understand it apart from the meaning given to it by God who created the universe.

Wisdom as part of Old Testament theology

We have come to the conclusion that wisdom does not

Figure 4. The perspective of salvation history

Salvation history (SH) concentrates on reality as represented by the redeeming work of God, Israel or the people of God, and the promised land. General considerations of God, mankind and the created order are on the horizon of its thinking but not absent.

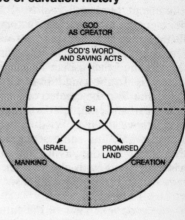

Figure 5. The perspective of wisdom

Wisdom (W) starts with the fear of the Lord, that is, from within the framework of salvation history. It assumes the perspective of salvation history while concentrating on those things which are on the horizon of salvation history. Its concern is God as creator, mankind and nature in general.

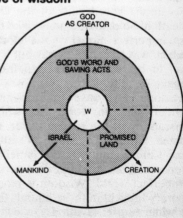

have a completely independent theology in the Old Testament. It is not a self-contained and alternative way of looking at God and reality. Rather, it complements the perspective of salvation history. Indeed, we should go further than that and say that wisdom is a theology of the redeemed man living in the world under God's rule. It is thus as much an aspect of kingdom theology as salvation history is. In the kingdom of God all relationships between God, man and the created order are perfectly restored. That is the final and completed expression of the kingdom in hope of which we still live. Wisdom in the Old Testament must be placed within the same structure of progressive revelation that exists for the saving acts of God. Broadly speaking, wisdom, along with every other dimension in the Bible, is revealed in three major stages:

a. Israel's history,
b. the prophetic view of the future kingdom, and
c. the fulfilment of these in Christ.

Wisdom was a part of Israel's life during the first of these stages, although it did not really flourish until the end of this period. It came into its own when the structures of the kingdom of God and of salvation had been revealed in the historical experience of Israel from Abraham to David and Solomon. The decline of the kingdom of Israel after the death of Solomon demonstrated that what had preceded was an imperfect model of the glory of the kingdom of God which was to come. It was but a shadow of the solid reality yet to be revealed. Nevertheless, this revelation of God's covenant and saving purposes is the presupposition of wisdom. The wise man is an Israelite who seeks to understand the world into which sin has intruded as a disruption of the perfect order, and within which God has acted, and is now acting, to restore that order. The fear of the Lord means that the Israelite had to see himself as a redeemed but still imperfect person, in a redeemed but still imperfect world. Wisdom is more concerned with contemporary life within these bounds than with the possibilities of a wider future salvation.

As the prophets spoke of Israel's failure, they spoke also of the covenant faithfulness of God. This meant that a future

restoration of the order was inevitable. From time to time
the prophets saw the significance of this for wisdom in that a
world made perfect would be a world fully displaying
wisdom both in the new creation and in man's relationships
to all things and to God. Thus part of the prophetic view of
the coming kingdom is that it is characterized by wisdom:

> The Lord is exalted, for he dwells on high;
> he will fill Zion with justice and righteousness.
> He will be the sure foundation for your times,
> a rich store of salvation and wisdom and knowledge;
> the fear of the Lord is the key to this treasure.
>
> (Isaiah 33:5–6)

This is the reversal of the terrible judgment pronounced
over the faithless Israel of the prophet's time:

> Their worship of me
> is made up only of rules taught by men.
> Therefore once more I will astound these people
> with wonder upon wonder;
> the wisdom of the wise will perish,
> the intelligence of the intelligent will vanish.
>
> (Isaiah 29:13b–14)[11]

There is also a significant concentration on the royal
wisdom of the future kingdom which recalls the place of
David and Solomon as fountainheads of wisdom. In the new
order the benign rule of God will be mediated by a messianic
prince who will be the paragon of wise men. It is David's
descendant who is to be the 'wonderful counsellor', and who
will establish and uphold God's kingdom with justice and
righteousness (Isaiah 9:6–7). When this Davidic shoot
sprouts from the stump of Jesse—

> The Spirit of the Lord will rest on him—
> the Spirit of wisdom and of understanding,
> the Spirit of counsel and of power,
> the Spirit of knowledge and of the fear of the Lord.
>
> (Isaiah 11:2)

---

11. See also Isaiah 47:10 where Babylon's wisdom is shown to be folly,
and Jeremiah 8:9; 9:23–24 (compare 1 Corinthians 1:31); 10:11–12.

The prophet goes on to describe this wise rule as both one of terrible judgment on the wicked who disrupt order, and one of restoration of universal harmony between man and beast. It is the time when the wolf lies down with the lamb, and when children can play amongst snakes without harm (vv. 6–9).

After these two Old Testament stages—wisdom in Israel's history, and wisdom in the prophetic kingdom of God—we come to the fulfilment of wisdom in Christ. Jesus brings to a climax the wisdom of Solomon and of all the wise men of Israel. He fulfils all that was foretold by the prophets of the wise rule of the messianic prince. He comes as the God-man in whom is all the wisdom of God perfectly relating to the wisdom of man. All things are reconciled to God through him and the harmony of creation is restored (Colossians 1:19–20). Thus God makes him to be wisdom for us (1 Corinthians 1:30).

In all three stages of revelation we see on the one hand a focal point in one person who mediates God's rule and wisdom, and on the other hand the people who engage in the task of learning wisdom in the framework of God's revealed wisdom. In the Old Testament the wisdom of God is not so clearly identified with salvation as in the New Testament where its greatest expression is in the gospel. Christ expresses for us both the wisdom of God mediated to us as gift, and the wisdom of man in its perfect expression of a life totally in harmony with its Creator. In bringing wisdom so totally within the ambit of salvation history in Christ, the New testament does not lose sight of the Old Testament's emphasis on wisdom which turns more to creation than salvation. God reveals to us with all wisdom and understanding the mystery of his will, which is his plan to unite all things in Christ (Ephesians 1:9–10). The gospel, God's wisdom, is the means by which God restores the order of all things.

Wisdom, then, presents a theology of creation as God's perfectly decreed order. It places man within a special relationship to that order; as the unique creature of God whose task is to take up God's command to have dominion. He is to engage the world in his doing and his thinking. He is to investigate, analyse, reason, invent and be creative within the bounds of his creatureliness. To be able to do this he must understand the meaning of the universe as it is revealed in God's prophetic word and saving action. Wisdom highlights the fact that man, the sinner living in a world of distorted relationships, is nevertheless responsible to live before God. His task is to understand life within the dynamic order which moves toward the consummation of God's redemptive plan. When man entered his social, cultural and intellectual infancy, he had before him the wisdom of God's word to light the way and to guide in the search for knowledge. And today, he looks down and into the creation, to the microcosmic realm of molecules, atoms and sub-atomic particles. He goes out to the moon, and reaches into the solar system with his space craft. He uses new forms of telescope to open windows into the heavens where distances are measured by the speed of light. He exercises dominion, albeit corruptly. But only those who fear the Lord and hear the wisdom of God will understand the ultimate significance of these things.

Wisdom is a theology of covenant adulthood, both corporate and individual. It recognizes that an important aspect of man's relationship to God is his responsibility to think and act in a world that is not, and was never meant to be, an open book nor a static, passive blob of matter. Within an ever changing world a wonderful and finely tuned balance exists between living things and the inanimate. Tiny ecosystems within larger ones, spread out until the entire planet appears as a self-contained life-support system that also interacts with the wider universe. If, from the scientific point of view, the meaning of the universe can only be guessed at, the fear of the Lord provides the answer. It is the Father's creation. As he made all things good, so he is re-creating all things according to a purpose known to us only through Christ.

Questions for study
1. How does Old Testament wisdom that makes no direct reference to God differ from the worldly wisdom that Paul condemns in 1 Corinthians 1–2?

2. How does the Old Testament theology of creation provide a bridge between wisdom and salvation history?

3. How would you explain the meaning of the biblical word *righteousness*, and how does wisdom relate to it?

4. What is the difference between natural revelation and natural theology, and how does wisdom relate to each?

11

Christ and the Perfection of Order

Summary

Wisdom is an important aspect of the person and work of Christ. Jesus embodied the true wisdom of both God and man. In his ministry he encountered the misconceptions which had thrown the Old Testament wisdom into crisis. Much of his teaching, including many of the parables, involves a confrontation with the false wisdom of the Jews of his day. The fact that Jesus fulfils wisdom means that the gospel presents a way of looking at the world. Thus we can identify an intellectual content of the gospel. Through the gospel God not only restores all relationships, but also reveals the nature of reality. Order and relationships that were the concern of wisdom are given their fullest and most perfect expression in Christ. Christ's being as God and man, and the perfect relationships he formed with all things, point to the unity and diversity of reality. The universe bears the stamp of its Creator who is 'one and many': trinity.

Return to the starting point

Now that we have considered wisdom in the context of Old Testament theology, we can move on to the point from which we started: Christ is our wisdom! I indicated at the beginning of this study that what the New Testament says about Christ as wisdom needs to be understood against the

Old Testament teaching on the subject. This is consistent with the method of biblical theology which begins with Christ as the fullest revelation of God to man and the one through whom we are turned from darkness to light. Thus Christ himself directs us to the Old Testament as that which speaks of him and which he fulfils. A Christian understanding of the Old Testament means that we read it in the light of its relationship to Christ.

The three stages of revelation dealt with in the previous chapter give a bird's-eye view of the biblical message from the salvation history perspective. But what of the wisdom perspective? Wisdom, as we have seen, stands firmly on the same foundation of creation as does salvation history. Furthermore, it presupposes God's self-revelation in salvation history, the true response to which is described as the fear of the Lord. True wisdom develops within the framework of salvation history and is unintelligible apart from it. Although wisdom does not deal with them in the same way as salvation history does, it acknowledges the creation of all things in orderly relationships, and the dislocation of these relationships through human sin. In being built on the fear of the Lord, it recognizes that disorder and chaos are not the norms for life but are the characteristics of the less than human existence which has resulted from our rebellion against God.

In Proverbs, Job and Ecclesiastes, along with the other wisdom works of the Old Testament, we can catch many glimpses of how the Israelite learned to cope with life during the period in which God was revealing the nature of his kingdom through Israel's historical experience and through the prophets. I have referred to the fact that the wisdom literature did not really flourish until the end of the era of God's revelation in Israel's history, that is, until Israel came of age under David and Solomon. During the period of historical decline when Israel as a nation came to mirror the reality of the kingdom of God less and less, wisdom had an important role in the daily life of the faithful. It was in that period that the major thrust of prophecy took on both a judgmental and promissory role. The prophetic view of the future which was expressed from Amos onwards projected the hope that the past glory would be restored along with the increase of glory in a nation made truly the people of God. There would also be a new glory in a restored world of right relationships. Thus, while the wise men of Israel were seeking to understand life in a world of confused order, the prophets were at the same time announcing a future day when true wisdom would characterize the nation. This prophetic view helps us to see how wisdom could be thought of within the processes of God's saving acts. A significant aspect of this prophetic view was the wisdom of the royal messianic rule.

Salvation history finds its goal and fulfilment in Christ. So too does wisdom. Three aspects of wisdom confront us in the New Testament. First, the Gospel narratives portray Jesus as the wise man who, in the form and content of many of his sayings, follows in the traditions of Israel's wisdom teachers. Secondly, Jesus goes beyond this actually to claim to be the wisdom of God. Thirdly, certain New Testament writers, notably Paul, understand the meaning of Christ's person and work in the light of certain wisdom ideas. Thus wisdom is seen as an important strand of Christology. We recognize also that to say that Jesus fulfils the Old Testament, including wisdom, means far more than that he is the end of a process and gains his meaning from what has preceded him. We should be clear about this point. The relationship of the two Testaments is such that while the New Testament presupposes the Old, the Old finds its real meaning in the New. As to the New presupposing the Old, we come to the New with the knowledge of the Old in order to understand much of its terminology and thought forms. But as to the New fulfilling the Old, we know what the Old is ultimately on about only as we see its goal in Jesus Christ.

We started with the gospel, with the testimony to Jesus of Nazareth, and found that it drove us back to the Old Testament in order to understand its presuppositions. But to go back to the Old Testament is like jumping into a swiftly flowing stream which carries us forward again to our starting point. There we see that all the various strands, images and perspectives of the Old Testament are drawn together in the person of Jesus.

The new crisis of wisdom

All four Gospels agree that the ministry of Jesus occasioned a rising tide of hostility towards him on the part of the Pharisees and Jewish religious leaders. We may describe this as a new crisis of wisdom. The first crisis arose because the old wisdom of Israel became fossilized and distorted in the thinking of many people so that it could not cope with new and contradictory experiences. Both Job and Qohelet rebelled against a simplistic notion of order which distorted the intention of Proverbs and prevented new insights from being added to those of the optimistic sages. The new crisis arose because of a fossilizing and distorting of the mainstream of Jewish thought so that a form of legalism became firmly established. Not only had the law gradually assumed an independence of grace, but the understanding of the future kingdom was bound by a particular and rather literalistic interpretation of the prophets.

The Scribes and the Pharisees displayed the same rigidity and dogmatism with their understanding of the wisdom of God as did the friends of Job. Thus they were incapable of accommodating the radical claims of Jesus. The old crisis was not a clash of empirical wisdom with speculative wisdom, but a clash of a distorted and shrivelled form of wisdom with something that did not fit its neat formulas. The new crisis was not a clash of the Old Testament with Jesus Christ, but a clash of a distorted form of Israel's faith with the unexpected and utterly surprising form of Old Testament fulfilment that Jesus announced in himself. The Old Testament prophetic faith should have led the Jews to a perception of the suffering messiah-prince. But Pharisaic Judaism had exalted law over grace, and thus lost sight of the need for a mediator. It submerged the great themes of the suffering servant under those of the glories of the restored land and people of Israel.

The constant use of wisdom forms by Jesus would seem to highlight this new crisis of wisdom. It is not only that the Gospels portray Jesus as the wise man above all wise men, but that he is presented as the teacher who uses and develops wisdom forms in a distinctive way. The actual

sayings of Jesus involve wisdom forms more than any other
type, so that we have much more to go on than the
statements which explicitly link Jesus with wisdom. The
Gospel narratives are full of sayings which have affinities
with older wisdom even though they may betray a process of
development beyond the major wisdom forms of the Old
Testament.

The most characteristic form of saying that Jesus used was
the parable. While recognizing that there is considerable
diversity in the form of the parables, we can identify about
seventy such sayings in the four Gospels.[1] It is sometimes
said that parables are earthly stories with a heavenly
meaning, thus suggesting that Jesus chose this medium in
order to make plain to all the reality of the spiritual realm
and of God's kingdom. In one sense this is true, but it is also
very misleading. There are several pointers to the fact that
the parables were a deliberate means of precipitating the
new crisis of wisdom by confronting the false wisdom of the
Pharisees. Thus we have the celebrated saying in Matthew
13:10–16 which follows the parable of the sower.[2] Jesus
concluded the parable with the provocative statement: 'He
who has ears, let him hear.' The disciples obviously felt that
this constant use of parables was a problem and asked him:
'Why do you speak to the people in parables?' Jesus replied:

> 'The knowledge of the secrets of the kingdom of heaven has
> been given to you, but not to them. Whoever has will be
> given more, and he will have an abundance. Whoever does
> not have, even what he has will be taken from him. This is
> why I speak to them in parables. Though seeing, they do not
> see; though hearing, they do not hear or understand.'

Although not drawn from the wisdom literature, this
passage shows one of the enigmas shared by wisdom and
prophecy. Isaiah's call was first to bring hardening to the
people who refused to turn to God. Jesus sees his parabolic
messages fulfilling the same role at a critical point in the

---

1. This includes certain sayings recorded in John who never refers to
them as parables.
2. Paralleled in Mark 4:10–12 and Luke 8:9–10.

history of salvation. Contrary to the popular idea about parables, Jesus says that he uses them because they create a division between those who are wise in their own eyes and the humble children of the kingdom. Of the latter, his disciples, he says, 'Blessed are your eyes, for they see, and your ears, for they hear' (v. 16).

In general, the nature of the parables was such that they were open to various interpretations. Only those whose understanding was enlightened by grace could perceive their application to the kingdom of God as it came with Jesus. Those who perceived this intended relationship were thus led to a greater understanding of Jesus. But for those, then or now, who see in the parables only illustrations of general religious truth, it is a matter of ears that hear not and eyes that see not.

This function of the parables, even though they now stand close to the redemptive history of the Bible, betrays their roots in the wisdom traditions. There are good reasons for maintaining that parables constitute a refinement of the Old Testament *mashal*. The fact that the Greek translation of the Old Testament (the Septuagint) uses *parabole* to translate *mashal* is suggestive. But the function of the parable to make comparisons after the fashion of proverbs is significant.[3] As with proverbial wisdom, the wisdom which comes in parabolic form is deceptive in that the uninitiated mistake parables for generalizations. Wisdom must penetrate to the meaning so that its specific application is perceptible. The parables can be understood only by those who recognize in Jesus the Messiah who now brings in the Kingdom of God.[4]

The ability of the new wise men, the disciples, to understand what Jesus was saying was strictly limited. But they had put themselves at the feet of *the* wise man and would learn from his instruction. At times they found his use of parables and metaphors difficult to grasp. Not only were

3. Amos Wilder, *Early Christian Rhetoric* (Cambridge: Harvard University Press, 1971), Ch. 5.
4. E. Hoskyns and N. Davey, *The Riddle of the New Testament* (London: Faber and Faber, 1958), p. 133.

they subject to their own humanness and the confusion of their sinfulness, but the truth was still in the process of being unveiled. Not until the gospel event was completed would they be able to see and understand the whole picture. John reminds us on a couple of occasions that it was after the event that the disciples understood certain matters in Jesus' life (John 2:22; 12:16). The disciples needed reminding that more was to come:

> I have much more to say to you, more than you can now bear. But when he, the Spirit of truth, comes, he will guide you into all truth. (John 16:12–13)

At one stage the disciples expressed relief that Jesus had stopped using figurative language and spoke plainly. Unhappily, though they had made progress, they did not really understand things as well as they thought (John 16:25, 29–32). To them the fear of the Lord was real, for in varying degrees they had perceived that Jesus was the one sent from God. A turning point came when Peter confessed, 'You are the Christ' (Mark 8:29). But it was only at Pentecost that the full significance of Jesus' person and work burst upon them.

The parables, though diverse in form, are relatively simple to identify in the Gospels. Less obvious are the proverbial forms of speech which occur frequently in the sayings of Jesus. It has been pointed out that some of the parables of Jesus actually illustrate Old Testament proverbs:[5]

> Do not exalt yourself in the king's presence,
> and do not claim a place among great men;
> it is better for him to say to you, 'Come up here,'
> than for him to humiliate you before a nobleman.
> (Proverbs 25:6–7)

> But when you are invited, take the lowest place, so that when your host comes, he will say to you, 'Friend, move up to a better place.' Then you will be honoured in the presence of all your fellow guests. (Luke 14:10)

---

5. William A. Beardslee, 'Uses of the Proverb in the Synoptic Gospels', *Interpretation* XXIV, January 1970, 61–73.

> And if you look for it as for silver
> and search for it as for hidden treasure,
> then you will understand the fear of the Lord
> and find the knowledge of God. (Proverbs 2:4–5)

> The kingdom of heaven is like treasure hidden in a field.
> When a man found it, he hid it again, and then in his joy
> went and sold all he had and bought that field.
> (Matthew 13:44)

Jesus also uttered proverbial sayings that have their counterpart in the book of Proverbs:

> If your enemy is hungry, give him food to eat;
> if he is thirsty, give him water to drink. (Proverbs 25:21)

> But I tell you, love your enemies and pray for those who
> persecute you. (Matthew 5:44)

> A man's pride brings him low,
> but a man of lowly spirit gains honour.
> (Proverbs 29:23)

> For whoever exalts himself will be humbled, and whoever
> humbles himself will be exalted. (Matthew 23:12)

Many other sayings of Jesus have a proverbial ring:

> Ask and it will be given to you; seek and you will find; knock
> and the door will opened to you. (Matthew 7:7)

> You are the salt of the earth. But if the salt loses its saltiness,
> how can it be made salty again? You are the light of the
> world. A city on a hill cannot be hidden.
> (Matthew 5:13–14)

> The Sabbath was made for man, not man for the Sabbath.
> (Mark 2:27)

It has long been considered by some scholars that the blessings and woes of the Bible have roots in wisdom.[6] In my

---

6. E. Gerstenberger, 'The woe oracles of the prophets', *Journal of*

opinion the case is not proven, especially as the word *woe* does not appear in the wisdom literature except in Proverbs 23:29, and (a different Hebrew word) in Job 10:15. Nevertheless, it is difficult to bypass the blessings and woes of Jesus in our consideration of wisdom. Many of them show the same concerns as the proverbial wisdom of the Old Testament. For example, the woes recorded in Luke 11:37–54 involve a series of contrasts between true righteousness and the feigned righteousness of the Pharisees. The whole episode is brought on by the failure of Jesus, before a meal, to fulfil the ritual expectations of a certain Pharisee. This new, unexpected behaviour contravened the Pharisees' rigid view of law which prevented them from seeing the offensive things that Jesus did as signs that the kingdom had come. They were so preoccupied with the shadows of the kingdom that they failed to see the reality when it was before their eyes. This event is another example of the crisis of wisdom. So serious is this failure to see the truth that it calls forth from Jesus the strongest expression of disapproval; the woe.

First there is a wisdom-like metaphor describing the Pharisees:

> Now then, you Pharisees clean the outside of the cup and dish, but inside you are full of greed and wickedness.
>
> (Luke 11:39)

Because they confuse ritual conformity with actual righteousness they are rejecting the very wisdom that Israel's laws were intended to express:

> You foolish people! Did not the one who made the outside make the inside also? But give what is inside to the poor, and everything will be clean for you. (vv. 40–41).

Then follow six woes, some of which make an explicit contrast of the folly of ritual legalism or pride, with the

Biblical Literature, 81, 1962, 249–263. See also Waldemar Janzen, 'ASRE in the Old Testament', *Harvard Theological Review*, 58, 1965, 215–226, and W. J. Whedbee, *Isaiah and Wisdom* (Nashville: Abingdon Press, 1971), p. 87–88.

wisdom of inner righteousness. Thus they tithe even the herbs of the garden while neglecting justice and love of God, or they desire the praise of men rather than the praise of God (compare Proverbs 25:6–7). These false teachers have repudiated the wisdom of God by killing the prophets. Now note the biting irony of the last woe:

> Woe to you experts in the law, because you have taken away the key to knowledge. You yourselves have not entered, and you have hindered those who were entering. (v. 52)

The opposite to the woe is the blessing. Jesus pronounced many blessings which, like the woes, occur in wisdom-like sayings. The most notable group, the Beatitudes, form the opening to the Sermon on the Mount. This, as we saw in Chapter 1, also ends with a wisdom comparison of the wise man and the fool,[7] and it contains many proverbial statements within it. The whole of the Sermon may thus be seen as a type of wisdom instruction which, if addressed to the multitude at large, throws the false path of the Pharisees into conflict with the wisdom of Jesus.

Enough has been said to indicate that Jesus deliberately chose the role of the wise man to complement his roles as prophet, priest and king. As the prophet he came not only to speak God's word of revelation, but to be the very Word incarnate by which alone we can know the truth. As the priest Jesus came to be the mediator between God and man, and to offer himself as the one true sacrifice for sin. As the king he came to bring in the glorious rule of God's kingdom. As the wise man he came as the very wisdom of God challenging the folly of a humanity that has turned its back on the word of God. He came to challenge the folly of every age, and to impart wisdom to those whom he would call to himself. He challenged the folly of the Judaism of his day and especially that of the Pharisees. He did this by showing up the assumptions of Torah-centred religion that had steadily lost sight of the dynamic nature of Israel's faith

---

7. There are overtones here of Proverbs 10:25, 'When the storm has swept by, the wicked are gone, but the righteous stand firm for ever.' See Beardslee, *op. cit.*, p. 65.

which propelled it towards the new age. The Jews continued to expect a new age, or at least a life after death, except for the Sadducees who seem to have lost faith in any vital new ordering of existence yet to come. In general, the expectations of the Jews left no room for a messiah like Jesus who did not move towards the kingdom as a present political reality. All four Gospels stress the growing tension between Jesus and the Jewish religious authorities. Some of the latter were nervous about Jesus because of a possible Roman reaction to any messianic movement which threatened the peace of the province. But the hostility of the Jews seems to have been due mainly to his teaching. He is shown to be constantly saying and doing things which excite the anger of the Jews. He challenges their claims to know the truth and to be its guardians. By appearing to flout the ritual laws so beloved by the Pharisees, Jesus was to them a blasphemer and an apostate. But, as the Gospels make clear, these very actions of Jesus point to the coming of the kingdom and the fulfilling of the Old Testament hopes. Not only did this occasion the hardening of the Jews, but for those that did believe it was still a matter of considerable surprise and wonderment.

The intellectual content of the gospel

On our journey through the wisdom of the Old Testament we have seen that it belongs to the young and simple (as well as to the experienced and the complicated). The prerequisite for wisdom is not a high I.Q. but the fear of the Lord. Now that we have returned to the New Testament we find the same perspective on wisdom; it is the fear of the Lord, or faith in Christ, rather than intellectual wizardry that is at the heart of it. Faith in Christ is accompanied by a new view of reality which Paul speaks of as the renewing of our minds (Romans 12:2). This is a normal part of being Christian. Thus, from the biblical point of view, the youngster who is intellectually 'slow' but who has a simple trust in Jesus as his Saviour, is wiser than the brilliant philosopher who, despite his intellectual powers, refuses the knowledge of God in his word.

In accommodating those who are decidedly not what we would call intellectuals, through lack of ability or opportunity, we nevertheless must not neglect the importance of the mind.[8] This is one of the lessons of wisdom. Unfortunately, there is a tendency among Christians, particularly those oriented towards the inner spiritual experience, to neglect the relationship of the gospel to the way we think. It is almost as if careful thought and reasoning play no part in being Christian. This is seen not only in peculiar views of guidance, but also in a distrust of theology and of any attempt to achieve precision in the exegesis and interpretation of the Bible. This kind of Christianity rarely challenges the non-Christian mind-set in any meaningful way.[9] Such challenges belong not only to place of higher learning, but also in the context of the ordinary man's work place. The unskilled worker and the shop-assistant also have an intellectual interpretation of reality to which the gospel must be addressed.

The intellectual content of the gospel signifies that the life, death and resurrection of Jesus as God's way of saving sinners is closely related to the meaning of the whole of reality. Furthermore, the gospel is God's way of revealing to us what this ultimate meaning is. Thus, Christians must accept the responsibility of developing a world-view which is meaningful in contemporary terms and which is consistent with the gospel. Obviously a universe which came into being from eternally existing matter, a universe not created but rather the result of chance plus time, and a humanity which is not responsible before God, are all ideas which clash violently with the fact that Jesus died for our sins. Unless the universe is the creation of a personal and eternal God, the gospel has no meaning at all.

In Old Testament wisdom there are two complementary ideas: God endows his people with wisdom as a gift, and this gift demands the responsive task of learning wisdom. Solomon's prayer for understanding was granted but, having

8. See John Stott, *Your Mind Matters* (Leicester: Inter-Varsity Press, 1972).

9. This is discussed in C. Van Til, *The Intellectual Challenge of the Gospel* (London: Tyndale Press, 1950).

been equipped with the divine gift, he engaged in the continuing task of learning, discovering, classifying, reasoning and making decisions. The gift should not be seen as a purely private and supernatural energizing of Solomon's thinking powers. Gift and task go hand in hand. That Solomon recognized the fear of the Lord, even though he later let this reference point slip out of focus, shows that his faith and the object of that faith were inseparable from his wisdom. In other words, Solomon's wisdom cannot be understood apart from all of his perceptions of the covenant and God's saving acts. What God has done for him under the covenant was the prior gift from which the gift of wisdom stemmed. In the same way that the gift of redemption demanded the task prescribed by the law, so the gift of wisdom demanded the task of learning and applying wisdom.

Jesus fulfilled the role of Solomon as the wise king of Israel. Solomon's wisdom was imperfect, but Jesus' wisdom was perfect. Solomon's perceptions of his relationship with the Father were marred by sin and ignorance, but Jesus had a perfect perception of all relationships. By being the perfectly wise man for us, Jesus is qualified to redeem us from sinful ignorance and its effects. Included in this redemptive process is the instruction of our minds. By what he was and did, Jesus shows us how things are in reality. Thus he patterns the reality of our relation to God, to others and to the world. We do not ignore his uniqueness as the God-man and Saviour of the world. We cannot imitate these attributes, but we can learn from the nature of the relationships that are actually restored to perfection in the person of Christ.

What, then, is the intellectual framework of the gospel? The Christian faith proclaims that the universe was created by God who is Trinity. The knowledge of God as Trinity comes to us as a result of the gospel. Once it was recognized that somehow Jesus was God come in human flesh, it was inevitable that a distinction would have to be made between him and the Father in heaven. The same distinction was also indicated by the reality of the Holy Spirit as divine person. God, it would seem is a community of being, three persons *and* one God. In the same way Jesus came to be perceived as communal in that he was two natures *and* one person. But this kind of relationship had been recognized as a reality in human and other relationships from earliest times in Israel. It was just that it had not been clearly understood with respect to the being of God.

The way God relates within himself as Father, Son and Holy Spirit is reflected in the relationships of the universe which he created. This is the question of order that exercised the wisdom writers. A particular form of the question is the relationship of the one and the many, the individual to all other individuals, and the one group (or class) to the many individuals. All the questions of human relationships that concern us are variations of the problem of the one and the many. All the questions raised in the wisdom literature are expressions of this concern. This is the problem behind the relationship of males to females in general, of husband to wife in particular, of parents to children, of believer to unbeliever, of worker to employer, of humans to animals, of humans to inanimate creation, and so on. The list is endless. But above all we seek to know the relationship of God to man.

In order to highlight the importance of a truly Christian approach to these matters let us first consider a couple of examples of where non-Christian thinking takes us. A humanist who rejects the possibility of God is left with only the results of blind chance in the shaping of the universe. If humanity is the outcome of natural selection, fortuitous mutation, or survival of the fittest, then all human relationships are cast in that mould. If the humanist is going to be consistent with his own premises he has no real basis for establishing right or wrong in human relationships. In our western society it would be true to say that humanists and non-Christians in general have actually used an ethical base which is borrowed from Christianity. Unhappily that is changing and ethics more consistent with humanism are becoming more and more prevalent. For example, abortion on demand expresses a survival of the fittest ethic which is totally at variance with the Christian view of human life and of man created in God's image. The modern sexual revolution shows a confusion which arises when the proper basis for ethics and human relationships is removed.

Another non-Christian view of reality is that of the Pharisaic Judaism that Jesus encountered. This is not a God-denying position in the sense of being atheistic. Furthermore, it shares its beginnings with Christianity in the same Scriptures of the Old Testament. Yet when Jesus, claiming to be the one to which the Old Testament points, made claims to oneness with God, the Jews were provoked to anger (e.g. see John 5:17–18). It may be that their convictions concerning the oneness of God made it difficult for them to accept the implication that God could have come in human flesh while still being the one who dwells above the heavens. But this was not because such a concept is inconceivable in the light of the Old Testament. The enduring statement of faith, still central to Judaism today, was the *Shema'* from Deuteronomy 6:4–5:

> Hear, O Israel: the Lord our God, the Lord is one. Love the Lord your God with all your heart and with all your soul and with all your strength.

Here, as we find it consistently throughout the Old Testament, God is proclaimed as one (Hebrew: *'echad*). The nature of God's oneness must be understood from the revelation of the whole Bible, but this word *one* does not rule out a complexity or plurality within the oneness. Thus, the same word is used of husband and wife becoming one flesh (Genesis 2:24), of Pharaoh's two dreams being one (Genesis 41:25), and of a nation gathering as one man (Judges 20:1).[10]

---

10. Gordon Jessup, *No Strange God* (London: Olive Press, 1976), p. 105. Jessup comments: 'It has been suggested, by at least one notable Jewish scholar and professor, that there was a time when Judaism could have accepted a Trinitarian doctrine of God. By the time of Maimonides, Christian anti-Jewish behaviour had made this emotionally impossible. From his time onwards it has also been intellectually impossible (except by the grace of God) for an Orthodox Jew to believe in a God whose Unity is so complex that it can also be called Trinity.' The reference to Maimonides is to a twelfth century AD Jewish philosopher who, in speaking of God, introduced the use of the Hebrew word *yachid*, which is related to *'echad* but which emphasizes the solitary nature of oneness.

The problem of one-and-many is illustrated in the confusion people experience over the use of collective nouns in English. It used to be taught that proper English usage demanded a singular verb with a collective noun: the committee *is* agreed, the team *is* playing well, the flock *is* following the shepherd. Test cricket commentators seem to have changed the rules in that they usually report that England (or Australia) *are* all out for a score of . . . The problem is that the idea of team is both singular (one team) and plural (many members). Logically it is the aspect we wish to stress that determines whether we think of it as singular or plural. But if we are to do justice to the reality of team-ness we somehow have to handle both the one-ness and the many-ness together.

We can press this same illustration further. The reference to England or Australia being in to bat is accepted without question. But England and Australia are never in, that is, neither a land nor a nation can play as a cricket team. England here means a team of eleven players who represent the nation. And while fifty thousand spectators in the stands must be clearly distinguished from the team that represents them (or else there would be chaos on the ground), yet such is the unity between spectators and team that, after it is all over, every one of those spectators will have in his mind, 'we won' or 'we lost'.

To return to the *Shema'*, the illustrations above help us to understand why Israel's conviction that God is one does not rule out the possibility that he is something greater than undifferentiated, solitary oneness. In fact, if God has indeed imprinted his character on the universe then at least it would be possible that somehow God is one and many, for that is what we see all around us. Every aspect of our experience makes sense only if we understand ourselves and all relations as expressing both unity and distinction. According to the New Testament, God as the source of this fact of reality is like that himself.

This doctrine of God's tri-unity begins with Jesus as the God-man. The incarnation is the supreme expression of this truth within our world of space and time. There are two distinct aspects to this. First, Jesus is both God and man. If someone, seeing Jesus walking along the road, had said, 'There's God', his statement would have been correct but inadequate. Likewise, if he had said, 'There's a man', this statement also would have been correct but inadequate. Until the two aspects are put together so that we say, 'There's the God-man', the truth is not only inadequate, it is actually distorted by being left out of its relationship to the other part of the truth.

This points us to the question of the kind of relationship existing between the two truths. If we say that because Jesus is both God and man, he must be two persons, then we are in error. He is, as theologians say, two natures in one person; he is uni-plural. At the fifth-century council of Chalcedon, after much controversy, the Christian church devised a manner of speaking which made it clear that we could not solve the mystery of uniplurality by simple logic (or any other kind of logic). Rather, to be true to the facts we must come to terms with the existence of the mystery. So, if Jesus is properly described as being both truly God and truly man, we recognize the unity of the two natures without confusing them, or, to put it the other way, we recognize the distinction of the two natures without separating them.

The second aspect of the incarnation is that it points us to God as Trinity. The numbers may differ, but the same kind of relationship exists here as in the person of Jesus. What Chalcedon said about the person of Jesus could be adapted to help us speak more accurately about the nature of God as Trinity.[11] We must always maintain the unity of God, so that

---

11. The so-called Creed of Saint Athanasius expresses the uni-plurality of the Godhead and of Jesus Christ. The creed is thought to pre-date the formula of Chalcedon (451 AD) as it presents a somewhat cumbersome expression of the doctrines. That it was thought suitable for the ordinary Christian's consumption is seen in the fact that the English Prayer Book directed that it be said on certain days at Morning Prayer in place of the Apostles' Creed. The wordiness of this creed illustrates the impossibility of giving adequate expression to uni-plurality. It can be found in the 1662 *Book of Common Prayer* under the heading 'At Morning Prayer' (immediately after Evening Prayer) and in *An Australian Prayer Book* (1978) on p. 625.

whatever he does, he does as Trinity; Father, Son and Holy
Spirit. On the other hand the distinctions must be maintained so that we do not simply interchange the three
persons in their distinctive roles.

One other point should be mentioned. Jesus expressed
the same uni-plural relationship between himself and the
Father.[12] This is similar to the relationship between his two
natures. Again it is a matter of both the oneness and the
plurality, the unity and the distinction. Jesus stressed the
distinction when he addressed the Father as 'Thou', or when
he spoke of the Father as 'greater than I'. But he also made
frequent assertions of unity such as 'I and the Father are
one', or 'He who has seen me has seen the Father'. Both sides
must be grasped if we are not to reach a false view of Christ.

All relationships express some kind of uni-plurality
through unity and distinction. We have seen that the prime
concern of wisdom is that of relationships and the order of
things in the universe. Christ fulfils for us the function of
wisdom by being the fullest expression of wisdom. Thus the
gospel event becomes for us wisdom in the sense that the
nature of order is revealed in Christ. His uni-plurality points
to that of the Godhead and thus to that of the universe which
bears the stamp of his nature. The wisdom literature constantly examines the unity and distinctions of relationships
which characterize the order within the universe. It is the
function of wisdom to perceive in any situation how to maintain the appropriate relationship of unity and distinction.
For example, in Proverbs 6:6 the industry of the ant, by
being an example to the lazy man, shows the kind of unity
that exists between the man and the insect:

> Go to the ant, you sluggard;
> consider its ways and be wise!

But another saying, Proverbs 26:14 warns that the lazy man
is in danger of taking unity to the point where there is no
distinction between him and a certain inanimate object:

---

12. John 14–16, Jesus' discourse about the giving of the Spirit, contains
frequent references to both unity and distinction of Father, Son and Holy
Spirit which compel us to recognize the tri-unity of God.

As a door turns on its hinges,
so a sluggard turns on his bed.

The gospel presses home this unity and distinction perspective by showing that this is the way the universe is because this is the way God is.

From this gospel-based perspective, the New Testament letters take up all kinds of human relationships in this light. In a practical way they show that the gospel provides the proper framework, the fear of the Lord, within which we pursue wisdom. An example of this is seen in Paul's discussion of the husband-wife relationship in Ephesians 5:21–33. This relationship is a reflection of the relationship between Christ and the Church, which in turn echoes the relationship between God and his people. It is significant that in this discourse Paul recalls Genesis 2:24 and its perspective of uni-plurality: 'the two will become one flesh.' We should note that unity-distinction is only one aspect of the relationship. We still have to take into account the characteristics of those persons or things that are relating. While unity-distinction characterizes all relationships, God and man can relate only *as* God and man. That will be very different from the relationship between husband and wife, which is different again from the relationship of brother and sister. That is why we stress that in the incarnation it is God relating to man. It is the nature of God, among other things, to be absolutely sovereign, while it is the nature of man to be absolutely responsible. They remain thus while relating perfectly in the one person Jesus Christ. Likewise, for a husband and wife to become one flesh does not mean that they lose their maleness or femaleness.

The fact that we cannot understand how there can be a uni-plurality in God or in Christ is only expressive of the real distinction between us, with our finite minds, and the infinite God. But that it *is* so is something we grasp because the Bible shows us that it is so. The examples given will suffice to show that there is a structure to all relationships that stems from the 'structure' of relationships within the communal oneness of God. The fear of the Lord as the beginning of wisdom points to the intellectual content of the gospel where we see Jesus Christ as the pattern of all truth.

The gospel of restored relationships

I want now to touch on another aspect of how wisdom
relates to the person of Christ. It is sometimes suggested that
Proverbs 8 involves a personification of wisdom which is
intimately related to God's creative activity. It is also
suggested that Paul points to this in some of his statements
about Christ as wisdom (e.g., 1 Corinthians 1:24,30). But it
is not at all clear that Proverbs 8 is a real personification,
that is, wisdom credited with a personal, independent
existence alongside of God. It seems more likely that it is a
poetic way of speaking about God's wisdom which is
expressed in the creation of the world.[13]

How, then, can we speak of Christ as the wisdom of God?
This is a complex question, and we shall focus on one aspect
of it. We have seen that wisdom in the Old Testament sits
very close to the doctrine of creation. We have also seen that
both wisdom and creation are closely related to salvation
history in their own characteristic ways. If we reduce these
three areas, wisdom, creation and salvation history, to their
bare skeletons, we find they all have the same underlying
structure. Creation is God bringing all things to be so that
there is God, mankind and the rest of creation, all relating
properly as God determines. Sin is seen to disrupt these
relationships in such a radical way that the only relationships
not dislocated are those within the Godhead. Salvation is
God's way of restoring all things to their proper order, so
that once again there will be God, man and the rest of
creation in proper relationships. Wisdom proceeds from the
basis of God's revelation of what these relationships once
were, and how God is restoring them to what they will be
again. Then it strives for knowledge and understanding of
where we are now, with the aim of knowing how to relate
properly to a world in flux. Thus wisdom is concerned with
the present relationships of God, mankind and the world,
not as a static reality, but as a reality which is moving
towards the restoration of all things. Creation, salvation
history and wisdom thus contain the same type of skeleton,

13. See James D. G. Dunn, *Christology in the Making* (London: SCM
Press, 1980), Ch. 5.

namely God, mankind and the world which together are presented as a peculiarly biblical understanding of the nature of reality, and of the relationships of everything in it.

The Bible thus presents us with at least two distinct, though related, perspectives of reality. These appear to diverge for a while, but are then brought back together in the person of Jesus Christ. Both perspectives deal with the same biblical raw material of reality and stand on the same base line of creation. Salvation history, as one perspective, embraces the whole history of a specific family of humanity which includes Israel. When we follow the sacred genealogy by way of Adam, Seth, Noah, Shem, Abraham, and Jacob, we are caught up in the manner of God's dealing with this family. God's acts are structured by covenant and redemption, promise of salvation and fulfilment. The sequence of events can also be reduced to basics:

a) Creation is God bringing all things into existence and into proper and harmonious relationship.

b) The fall of mankind through Adam's sin results in all relationships being dislocated and confused.

c) Salvation is God's action to bring all things back to proper relationships.

d) Jesus Christ is God and man in right relationship in that he is the only sinless man since the fall. Jesus' human nature means that he also participates in the physical creation. Thus we can say that the person of Jesus was, for the first time since the fall, a true expression of God, man and created order in right relationships.[14]

Salvation history culminates in the gospel, but at the same time embraces the subsequent history of mankind until Christ returns. We are bound to express the whole New Testament perspective in relation to Jesus Christ and to the Old Testament. Furthermore, we are justified in using the concept of *order* to signify the ordered reality of God, man and world. Thus we can restate the progression of salvation history which is summarized above in the following way:

---

14. See *Gospel and Kingdom* where salvation history is worked out in some detail as God's people in God's place under God's rule. This summary of the components of the kingdom of God is simply another way of expressing God, man and created order in right relationships. The kingdom concept is a model of the right relationships that God intends.

a) Creation: *order*.
b) Fall: dislocation of *order*.
c) Covenant: promise of restored *order*.
d) Exodus: a redemptive pattern of *order* being restored.
e) Kingdom of David and Solomon: a pattern of the *order* to come.
f) Jesus Christ: the reality of *order* representatively established.[15]
g) Christ's kingdom revealed at his return: *order*.

The perspective of wisdom takes its departure from the same starting point as salvation history, that is, creation. It presupposes the revealed significance of salvation history while focusing more on the creation than on redemption. It comes to its culmination in Jesus of Nazareth. In our study of wisdom we have seen that the question of the order of relationships is paramount. Again, using the concept of *order* to signify God, man and world in right relationships, we can summarize wisdom's perspective:

a) Creation: *order*.
b) Sin and folly: dislocation of *order*.
c) Wisdom is understanding the present confused *order,* and the future restored *order,* so that one can live according to what is real.
d) Jesus Christ is made wisdom, that is, *order* for us.

We can see that wisdom and salvation history are two sides to the one reality. This is not a static reality, but dynamic, moving from original perfection, to disruption, through restoration to ultimate consummation and perfection. Salvation history has a strong eschatological emphasis in that it continually envisages the end or goal of the process. Wisdom is not eschatologically oriented for the most part.

---

15. When Jesus brought in the kingdom at his coming it was he who was the kingdom. It is important to understand that God restored all things *in him* as the means of restoring all things in themselves. Jesus came as our representative as well as our substitute. All the right relationships of reality actually existed in Jesus of Nazareth; he was the one who stood for the many.

Its concentration is on the life we live in the present, and the relationships that we must pursue in a fallen and confused world. Its eschatology is implicit for its goal is life, and life ultimately is lived in perfect relationship to God, fellow man and the universe. In the framework of salvation history the concern of wisdom is for an understanding of where the one who fears the Lord is now, and what his relationship should be to a world under judgment but also under promise.

To conclude this discussion we may sum up the meaning of Christ as the wisdom of God. First, Christ as eternally God was present at the creation and active in the expression of God's wisdom. Secondly, the wisdom of God was such that Jesus Christ in the gospel event was the eternally devised plan of God upon which creation was based. Thirdly, the redemptive work of God, for the benefit of a sin-laden creation, was achieved not only by an atoning death, but by the new creation in Christ's person where God, man and the created order perfectly related. Fourthly, the disruption of sin was of such a nature that it brought all human thought about ultimate reality into opposition to the actual truth. Fifthly, God gives true wisdom to his people as a gift when he sends Christ into the world. Christ justifies our confused wisdom by having perfect human wisdom for us. He sanctifies our confused wisdom by patterning the truth and by giving his Holy Spirit to lead us in the paths of that truth. Finally, he will glorify our wisdom when we are renewed through our resurrection and are made to reflect his character perfectly.

Questions for study
1. In what way were the parables of Jesus the new wisdom sayings, and in what way did this wisdom clash with that of the Jews of Jesus' day?
2. How does the gospel—the life, death and resurrection of Jesus—provide Christians with the only valid foundation for wisdom and an understanding of the universe?
3. How does the gospel bring together the two Old Testament perspectives of wisdom of salvation history?

12

Christians and the Transformation to Order

Summary

Since wisdom has been fulfilled in the person and work of Jesus, Christians must read the Old Testament wisdom literature in the light of this fulfilment. Wisdom always functions within the framework of God's saving acts and word. Christ not only died to save us, but was also the perfectly wise man of God living the absolutely responsible life. He lived this life in our place that we might be accounted wise before God. His life was also the example of true wisdom so that we might learn wisdom from him. The overview of wisdom in the Bible provides us with a base for our decision-making. Guidance is primarily directed at the responsibility of Christians to make decisions which conform to reality as it is revealed in the gospel.

Interpreting Old Testament wisdom

Given the distinctive perspective of wisdom in the Old Testament, does it require a special approach to its interpretation? In the previous chapter I pointed to the manner in which the real meaning of wisdom is linked to the person and work of Jesus Christ. This means that he cannot be bypassed when we are seeking to interpret Old Testament wisdom texts. The interpretation of any text of the Bible begins with its exegesis. Exegesis aims at finding out what the text meant in its original biblical context. Then, if we are to understand how the text relates to us as Christians, we must first understand how it relates to the gospel. Hermeneutics, or interpretation, means asking what the text means when seen in its proper relationship to the gospel.

Wisdom is tied to the same two reference points as is salvation history, namely, creation and the new creation in Christ. Furthermore, it is practised on the presuppositions of revelation in salvation history. Thus we would expect the interpretation of wisdom to proceed on much the same basis as the interpretation of salvation history texts. Essentially, our method of interpretation is our response to the nature of the Bible as a whole, taking into account both the unity of the Bible and the diversity of expression within that unity. Without some attention to the theological unity of the Bible it is not possible to appreciate the important relationships between the various stages of biblical revelation.

Our brief excursion into the wisdom sources of the Old Testament has concentrated on understanding how wisdom was to be pursued. Of necessity we had to forgo the detailed exegesis of the texts. The Christian Bible student can approach such exegesis with confidence that it will yield many insights into authentic Christian existence. To arm ourselves with these insights can only be beneficial, provided that we understand how the wise men meant them to function in the learning of wisdom. The other qualification is that we always recognize the incomplete nature of the Old Testament without the New.

In order to understand what a particular text meant in its original context, we need to consider both its historical and theological context. We must think our way into the situation of the original hearers or readers, and how they would have been expected to understand the text against their contemporary situation. The process of moving from the text to Jesus Christ depends upon where the text stands in the historical progression of God's revelation.

Wisdom expresses the existence of God's people at the climax of the period from Abraham to Solomon during which the kingdom of God is given expression in the historical experience of Israel. Wisdom continues as a significant area of Israelite thought after the historical

decline of the kingdom and right up to the era of the New
Testament. In chapter 4 we saw that wisdom flourished from
Solomon's time as an expression of the nation's coming to
maturity. Wisdom texts express the responsible humanity of
the people within the framework of God's revelation of his
kingdom. Wisdom thus reflected the human task of the
cultural mandate which had been given to Adam, but which
now operated within the political and earthly reality of the
kingdom in an unredeemed world. The fact that the people
of God lived then, and continue to do so now, in an
unredeemed world, raised all kinds of questions about the
kind of responses the redeemed should make to that which is
redeemed and that which is not redeemed.

God created human beings to function by the integrating
of two sources of truth. These are not equal sources which
operate side by side, but they are complementary. The first
is revelation through word from God. As a rational thinking
being, man is nevertheless incapable of knowing of himself
what is necessary to be known in order to interpret the world
around him. A rational and personal God has made man in
his image, including his rational-personal nature, to respond
to word revelation from God. Through this revelation man
receives the reference points he needs for an understanding
of relationships. In short, God reveals to man something of
the nature of the order in the universe. The second source of
truth is the combined operation of senses and reason.
Reason is not in itself a source of truth but a way of
programming information. The reason must first be com-
pliant with the truth of revelation if it is to process correctly
the information of our senses. That is why geniuses can in
biblical terms be fools. The way our reasoning operates is
not primarily a function of how clever we are, nor of how
much information we have managed to cram into our minds.
Rather it is a moral choice either to be independent of God
or to be subject to him in our thinking as well as our doing.
The moral choice to be independent of God was made in
what we refer to as the fall of man. Only the regenerative
power of gospel and Holy Spirit can enable us to make the
second and correct choice to submit to God.

Revelation is thus pre-eminent. God must address us and

define our humanity in relation to his being and to the world. Knowing God and knowing ourselves in this relationship are the prerequisites for the pursuit of understanding of the details of human experience. In Eden God addressed Adam and defined his cultural task and the bounds of his freedom. The very fact that God so spoke to his creature also defined the proper relationship between God and man. In the fallen world in which salvation history operates, God addressed his people by covenants of promise and law, both of which were linked to the acts of redemption in Israel's history. Israel's cultural task, of which wisdom is a principal expression, needed the revelation of God if it was to be understood and pursued. Now Christ has come as the fullest and most perfect word of God to man. By Christ God is interpreting the meaning of the universe, of our world and of the whole history of the human race. Christ interprets you and me so that we do not have to flounder in the ambiguity of our existence. He reveals to us what we need to know in order to get on with the business of living as responsible Christians.

In applying these broad principles to the book of Proverbs we begin by asking how it functioned in its original context. How did it function, that is, in instructing the people of God about their relationship to God, each other and the world? This is a theological question because *all* relationships involve our relationship to God. Proverbs highlights the practical side of learning how to relate to everything. It stresses the responsible task of the life of faith. Its theological function is to provide us with insights into how we translate our relationship to God into right relationships to man and the world. But because it emerged from the pre-Christian context of the Old Testament, its perception of relationships is limited by the incomplete nature of the revelation of God in the Old Testament.

The Old Testament prophets reveal a future kingdom in which the people of God will live in perfect relationships to each other and the world. Central to this perfection of wisdom among the people is the fact that the messianic king will be the living example of all true wisdom. But the reality of the kingdom does not mean that there will be no task in wisdom. Ignorance and imperfection in the knowledge of

God, along with sinful hardness of heart towards God's revelation, will be removed. The people of God will be perfectly conformed to God's will through a renewal of their nature (Jeremiah 31:31–34; Ezekiel 36:25–28). The responsible task of wisdom is demanded not because we are sinful, but because we are finite creatures of God. The cultural mandate was given to Adam in his innocence and not subsequent to the fall.

The responsible task of Proverbs is given its full and perfect expression by Jesus. This fulfils the prophetic expectation of the perfectly wise messianic king. As tempting as it is to rush from the texts of Proverbs to an application in our Christian life, we must discipline ourselves to relate our texts first of all to their fulfilment in Christ. Jesus in every way fulfils God's requirements for Israel. He was the perfectly wise man of God living the absolutely responsible life before his heavenly Father. In his perfectly human existence he lived according to his true perception of reality, making right decisions in the right place and at the right time. In all this he constantly lived as the one who perfectly feared the Lord. Thus, in our application to ourselves of the individual textual units of Proverbs, we need to be aware of the meaning of the gospel for our human existence. We cannot simply apply proverbial wisdom out of the Old Testament to ourselves as if we had never heard of Jesus Christ. Wisdom points to righteousness, but we know that Jesus' life was lived for us in order to provide a perfect righteousness for us that counts for our acceptance with God. Jesus justifies our feeble attempts to live wisely by being what we should be but cannot. Thus, God regards all believers as having the very wisdom of Christ. In other words, Christ has been made wisdom for us (1 Corinthians 1:30).

Moving a text via the gospel to ourselves has a transforming effect on the significance of that text. The fear of the Lord is given its specific and definitive meaning in terms of faith in the person and work of Jesus Christ as our Saviour. The intellectual content of the gospel illuminates the nature of the order within the universe with a clarity that did not belong to Old Testament revelation. It is here that the New Testament teaching of the Holy Spirit's work should be understood. Spirit and gospel go hand in hand, for it is the Spirit's principal work to apply the gospel of Jesus to the hearts and minds of God's people. The New Testament never suggests that the Spirit takes over our humanity. This would be a total negation of the nature of the gospel which is to restore our true humanity, not to remove it. The doctrine of creation establishes that there is a real distinction between God and man that must be maintained in the order of things. When it is suggested in any way that our humanity is absorbed by the Spirit of God this order is destroyed. Furthermore, the reason for Christ's coming in the flesh as true man is dissolved if God's purpose is to absorb us into his being. Salvation means the humanizing of man not his deification (or divinizing). Our unity with God lies in our being created in his image and reflecting his character. Our distinction from God lies in the fact that our destiny is to remain God's greatest creation and to live in response to his revelation of himself to us. All the wisdom literature is eloquent of these facts and explores their implications in life.

The differences between Proverbs, Job and Ecclesiastes are found mainly in their distinct emphases. Proverbs emphasizes the practicalities relating to observable order. This order is not self-interpreting; it needs God's revelation to interpret it. Job and Ecclesiastes emphasize the infinite greatness of God and of his wisdom. Consequently man is cut down to size and thereby discovers that his real humanity is not diminished by the recognition that he relates to God on an unequal footing. The mystery of order points to the comforting fact that God is infinitely greater than our minds can comprehend. Both Job and Qohelet invite an openness to the sovereignty of God and thus urge trust in him. Again we see that the wisdom of these books is given its purest expression in the person of Christ. All the tribulations of the Son of man were an assault upon the orderliness of his God-man relationship. But even the tribulation of the cross did not destroy his trust in the Father. Finally the resurrection demonstrated that the God-man relationship cannot be destroyed even by the intrusion of the ultimate disorder: death.

The gospel thus transforms all the wisdom of the Old Testament by showing its place in the ultimate destiny of

God's people. The gospel does not thereby render the Old Testament material superfluous for it constantly presupposes it. The New Testament does not go over old ground but shows how the old ground is to be understood and applied. Because Christ is the perfect expression of every facet of human wisdom in the Old Testament, he is able to be the grounds of our acceptance with God. Then he shows us the goal of our continual growth towards conformity to his character. Because he has become our wisdom we of necessity must study the Old Testament wisdom in the light of his fulfilment. The wisdom literature in its own distinctive way steers us towards responsible Christian living which applies the reality of Christ to every level of human existence. On the one hand it gives us the perception to make sense of our world, and on the other hand it strengthens our trust in God in the face of things we cannot make sense of. As we pursue wisdom in this gospel-centred way, we discover more and more how Christ is both the starting point and the goal.

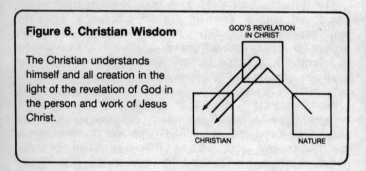

Figure 6. Christian Wisdom

The Christian understands himself and all creation in the light of the revelation of God in the person and work of Jesus Christ.

GOD'S REVELATION IN CHRIST

CHRISTIAN

NATURE

The gift of wisdom

What does the gift of wisdom entail for the Christian? In the Old Testament wisdom as gift appears to be available to all, yet there is clearly a special gifting of certain people for specific tasks. The same distinction appears in the New Testament. In the gospel every Christian has wisdom, but there is also that gift of wisdom which is a special manifestation of the Spirit (1 Corinthians 12:8). The specific gift must be examined in the light of the general gift given to all Christians.

The objective gift

I have indicated my understanding of the gift of wisdom to Solomon as something wider than the subjective enabling or mental power to perceive and know in a special way. The subjective aspect went hand in hand with wisdom as an objective gift. This lay in the revelation of God in the 'out there' events of salvation history. I would class the prophetic word which interprets these events as objective in the same way that the Bible is objective for us. For the Christian the objective gift of wisdom is the person and work of Christ. We cannot separate this from the whole biblical testimony of saving history because the entire Bible finds its ultimate meaning in the gospel. There are a number of New Testament references that make wisdom the equivalent of gospel so that he who possesses the gospel, truly believing it, possesses wisdom. For example, Stephen's wisdom in disputing with the Hellenists is reasonably inferred to be his ability to proclaim the gospel (Acts 6:10). It is an instance of that which Jesus promised in Luke 21:12–15, namely, the wisdom to bear testimony. Such testimony in the New Testament usually means testifying to the saving acts of God in Christ.

Essentially, the objective gift of wisdom is the self-revelation of God by which the people of God gain their bearings. Christians do well when they acknowledge that the Bible is wisdom for us. They do even better when they understand that the whole Bible finds its fulfilment in the gospel event. Thus, objective wisdom is the wisdom of God being shared with us through the revelation in the Bible of God's saving purposes in Christ. So, says Paul, the riches of God's grace, the benefits of the gospel, are lavished upon us with all wisdom and understanding (Ephesians 1:8). The saving activity of God, as it is proclaimed to the world, becomes an objective demonstration of the wisdom of God to the whole universe (Ephesians 3:8–10). It is an objective wisdom when the brethren teach and admonish one another according to the word of Christ in the gospel (Colossians 3:16). Likewise, it is an objective wisdom that we have already considered as the intellectual content of the gospel.

The subjective gift

The gospel as the wisdom of God ought to be our guide. The gospel is objective in that it is 'out there'. The finished work of Christ was effected entirely without our participation. But this 'out there' gospel must be applied to the sinner. It must become a part of his perceived world as something that applies to him and demands his involvement through faith and repentance. This subjective awareness that Jesus' life and death is 'for me' is a self-conscious going out from one's self to relate to the objective. The subjective perception of the gospel is never something that is wholly within me. It is always a response of what is in me to that which is out there. The gospel is always the same: it is Jesus Christ, the same yesterday, today and for ever (Hebrews 13:8). Our subjective perceptions of the gospel will vary from person to person. Many factors are involved such as how clearly and meaningfully the gospel is communicated, as well as our own background, training, and temperament. None of these has a predictable bearing on the response since it is the sovereign work of God through the power of the gospel to subdue whom he will. The grace of God in the gospel is the sovereign working of God by which the objective facts of the gospel become the subjective reality for the believer without ever losing their objective nature. Grace is gift as the gospel exemplifies it. The response to the gospel is the life of faith, the life of practical Christian wisdom. This is task. Gift and task can never be separated, for this is how God relates to his people.

I have risked labouring this matter because of its importance. The pattern of wisdom in the Old Testament conforms to the New Testament pattern of the responsible life of faith: gift and task. There are, however, some passages relating to the gift of wisdom that seem to emphasize the gift more than the task. Joseph is a case in

point. In rejecting von Rad's contention that the Joseph
narrative in Genesis 37–45 is a piece of wisdom literature
(see chapter 9), we cannot overlook the references to
wisdom within it.[1] Although Joseph is not referred to as
receiving the gift of wisdom, he does what the wise men of
Egypt could not do, that is, interpret the dreams of Pharaoh.
It is Stephen (Acts 7:10) who recalls Joseph as being given
wisdom by God so that he became Pharaoh's right-hand
man. While this wisdom would probably have included
interpretation of dreams, it is described more as a general
ability than as direct supernatural knowledge. Joshua's
wisdom was of a similar kind, although it came as a result of
the laying on of hands (Deuteronomy 34:9). It was a
charismatic gift for leadership in much the same way that
Solomon's was. In all, the gift and the task went hand in
hand, but with Joseph there was a gift of direct knowledge
through a supernatural revelation from God.[2]

The other major passages in which wisdom involves the
supernatural gift of knowledge relate to Daniel. The
narrative of Daniel 2 contains many close parallels to the
Joseph story. In both, the Israelites are captives among
foreigners. Both involve the dreams of foreign kings which
their own wise men fail to interpret. The dreams are from
God and only he can interpret them through his own wise
men. When the dreams are interpreted, the outcome has
saving significance for the people of God, a point which is of
utmost importance for the understanding of these events. I
stress that because all events of saving significance in the Old
Testament point towards Jesus Christ in the gospel event.
Their fulfilment is in what Jesus did for us rather than in
similar events in our own experience. The revelation of

---

1. The fact that Joseph acts as a wise man does not make the narrative a
wisdom story as von Rad suggests, any more than the references to
Solomon's wisdom in 1 Kings 3–10 make that narrative the work of a wise
man. These are narratives and not specially contrived compositions for
imparting wisdom.
2. All modern psychological theories of dream interpretation work
from some concept of cause and effect. What a person dreams is somehow
related to factors in his past, including how he has come to think about the
future. There would be no question of the prediction of future events such
as we see in Joseph.

dreams to Joseph and Daniel are more in the stream of
salvation history than of wisdom as practical living. Such
saving revelation reaches its fulness in Jesus Christ. Without
saying that God would not or could not make such direct
revelations to Christians today, we must assert that any such
revelation in the present would be of a different order from
that of the Old Testament revelations, since we now have
God's final word in Christ.

I conclude from all this that there is little in the Old
Testament, either in the narratives about the wise men, or in
the wisdom literature itself, to support the idea that a gift of
wisdom in the New Testament would consist of some fresh
supernatural revelation from God. To this we must add also
that there is no hint of such an idea in the extensive
treatment of wisdom in 1 Corinthians 1–2, which surely must
be definitive for the understanding of the significance of 1
Corinthians 12:8. Taking all the evidence of the nature of
wisdom in both Old and New Testaments, it is more realistic
to conclude that Paul is speaking of a God-given ability to
apply the meaning of the gospel in specific real life
situations. It presumably is to be distinguished from the
wisdom that belongs to all Christians, but probably only in
degree. The normal Christian experience would be that of
steady growth towards maturity through a willing involvement in the task of learning wisdom. The special gift of
which Paul speaks may well be demonstrated in a maturity
that is far beyond a person's years of Christian experience.

One problem of Paul's list of gifts in 1 Corinthians 12:4–11
is that it appears to distinguish the message of wisdom from
the message of knowledge. In most Old Testament contexts
wisdom and knowledge are almost synonymous, or at least
overlap to a greater or lesser degree. Even the skill of the
craftsman, which accounts for the uses of the word *wisdom*
in Exodus, has *knowledge* as a synonym.[3] If Paul intends a
distinction he has not explained what it is. It is important in
this discussion that we recognize what the gifts of wisdom
and knowledge almost certainly are not. Whatever they are,
they will not usurp the supreme place of Jesus Christ, or that

---

3. Exodus 31:3; 35:31.

of the canon of Scripture which testifies to him, in making known to us all that we need to know in order to make sense of ourselves and the world around us. Nor will they displace our task of using our brains and sanctified common sense. This does not rule out the possibility of such gifts being displayed as a manifestly supernatural ability to penetrate to the reality of any given situation.

Wisdom in James

The Epistle of James has long been considered as a work that is heavily influenced by Israelite wisdom. In some respects, James fulfils a role in the New Testament similar to that of Proverbs in the Old Testament. There are some obvious parallels in the way James exhorts the Christian to gain true wisdom. There are some problems with James, as is commonly recognized, not least of which is the lack of reference to the gospel. It would be difficult to reconstruct the nature of the gospel from this epistle beyond the fact that Jesus Christ is the Lord of glory and will return to judge the world. (Though James is far more explicit in his references to salvation history than 3 John where Jesus is not even mentioned.) Few would accept the view that James deliberately contradicts Paul in his treatment of faith and works (James 2:14–26), and what he says is consistent with the wisdom view of gift and task. So, to begin with, we note that James, like the wisdom literature of the Old Testament, makes few explicit references to God's saving acts but clearly presupposes them.

A second characteristic of this epistle is its lack of any theme or development. There are a number of practically oriented sections dealing with a variety of subjects relating to daily life. But it would be as erroneous to conclude of James that it is not theological as it would be of Proverbs. James writes as a Christian whose faith in the Lord of glory presupposes the life, death and resurrection of Jesus. The wisdom characteristics of James are not confined to the discourses on the subject (i.e. 1:5–8; 3:13–18). He everywhere displays the concerns of old wisdom as they would exist for first-century Christians.

The contrast in James between earthly wisdom and

wisdom from above is intensely practical. Every good gift is from above, that is, comes from God (1:17). Wisdom is one such gift and shows itself in the good life (3:13). It is pure, peace-loving, considerate, submissive, merciful, bearing good fruit (3:17). It is not unreasonable to suppose that what follows in James 4 and 5 (and perhaps what precedes) is the detailing of such wisdom in certain areas of life. James speaks of wisdom as gift and task which are based on the fear of the Lord, that is in his terms, faith in Jesus Christ the Lord of glory. There is no hint of a special charismatic gift of wisdom. Wisdom belongs to all and, indeed, it manifests itself in good works which witness to the reality of faith.

Decisions

As I stated in chapter 1, this book is not primarily about guidance and decision making. If we wanted a comprehensive treatment of the subject of guidance we would have to range far wider than the wisdom literature. Wisdom, however, is an important dimension in the matter. Many of the hang-ups people have about making decisions could be avoided by means of the perspective given by the subject of wisdom.

If we are to understand the biblical view of guidance, we need to look at it in the context of the progressive nature of revelation. The truth of God's revelation comes by stages until it reaches the full intensity of the light of the knowledge of God in Christ. There are two things to be said about guidance in this biblical framework. First, guidance of individuals by direct means of dreams, visions and prophetic word decreases as the repository of God's revealed will grows. This does not mean that such direct and supernatural guidance necessarily ceases once the canon of Scripture is completed, but it does mean that the likelihood of God adding to his final word in Christ recorded in the New Testament is very remote indeed. Secondly, I believe it is accurate to say that every case of special guidance given to individuals in the Bible has to do with that person's place in the outworking of God's saving purposes. To put it another way, there are no instances in the Bible in which God gives special and specific guidance to the ordinary believing Israelite or Christian in the details of their personal existence.

It was, in fact, in Israel come of age that we saw wisdom flourish as the practice of prudence in decision making among other things. Thus, we may justifiably say that a very important aspect of God's guidance in the Bible is that he refuses to guide us in every detail of existence beyond giving us the framework of his general will and purpose. The wisdom literature contributes very greatly to the overall impact of the Bible in establishing that God has given his children the freedom to make real choices between real options. None of this negates God's sovereignty, but it does highlight our redeemed humanity. It ought to be very clear by now that any notion that God removes the responsibility of decision making from us by some kind of perceptible inner (or even external) guidance simply does not accord with what is being said in the wisdom literature. It is also a denial of the biblical teaching of our humanity restored in Christ.

The Bible shows us the overall sovereign will of God in that all things will be brought to praise him. Within this will there is much that we cannot comprehend or which is not revealed to us. Job and Ecclesiastes point us to such mysteries as evil and suffering. Yet we know that these too will be made to praise God. The clearest example of this is seen in the crucifixion, the ultimate assault upon God by devil and man. Yet it was ordained by God as the means of saving God's people and of restoring universal order (Acts 2:23; 4:27–28).

Within this all-embracing sovereign will is the specific will of God revealed in the gospel. This is the will of God to save a people for himself and to bring them to glory in a regenerated universe. God has revealed to us his purpose in Jesus Christ. We know his will for us, namely, to conform us to Christ's image (Romans 8:29). This primarily is where guidance in the Bible is directed. It is impossible for God's people to miss out on this will of God for them because Christ will lose none of those given to him by the Father, and he will raise them up on the last day (John 6:35–40). We cannot miss out on God's best since we are possessed by Christ and will be like him.

But how does God bring us to this goal? Paul sums it up in terms of the Christian's growth in holiness: 'It is God's will that you should be holy' (1 Thessalonians 4:3). We know that we will be brought to the goal, but none of us can predict the path along which we will go. There are two possible ways of conceiving of this progress from conversion to glorification. The first is the special guidance approach which assumes that God has not only mapped out all the details of our lives but that we must discover them through special guidance. Thus we must seek God's guidance for every specific instance if we are not to miss out on his purpose for us. The Bible knows nothing of this, and in any case, it cannot work. It is tailor-made to produce a lot of anxiety-ridden Christians who are unsure about God's guidance with regard to which foot to put first.

The second approach to guidance is the wisdom way. That is, God has given us the framework within which to make our decisions for life. In the gospel lie all the principles needed for us to make wise and responsible decisions. In being urged to use our God-given brains to make decisions which are consistent with the gospel, we recognize that many situations, even those of great importance, present us with two or more options to choose from, none of which needs to be more acceptable than the others.

In the course of his daily decision making, the Christian can rest assured that he will not miss out on God's best. Through momentary insanity or stupidity he may choose a course of action that results in a lot of trouble, even tragedy. But even that cannot permanently remove him from the ultimate purpose of God. We all have much to repent of daily, and wiser (more gospel-directed) decisions would keep us from causing ourselves and others much hurt. Proverbs is largely directed to that end. The perspective of wisdom as gift and task is seen in Paul's saying which, for aptness of translation, I quote from J. B. Phillips's version:

So then, my dearest friends, as you have always followed my advice—and that not only when I was present to give it—so

now that I am far away be keener than ever to work out the
salvation that God has given you with a proper sense of awe
and responsibility. For it is God who is at work within you,
giving you the will and the power to achieve his purpose.
(Philippians 2:12–13)[4]

Paul is saying here that the Christians at Philippi must stop
depending on him to make their decisions for them. They
themselves must work out the implications of their salvation
into daily living. This is the task every Christian has in
response to the love of God shown to us in Christ. Notice
Paul's reassurance. God is working in us in a way that affects
both our willing and doing. God does not make our
decisions for us, but as we struggle to understand the world
in the light of revelation, God is at work in the decision-
making of all his people, working through our thinking and
willing in order to bring about our sanctification.

Christian wisdom in the technological age

I would like to conclude this discussion with a comment on
wisdom and technology. A simple definition of technology is
man's ability to make things. This is the very thing that the
word *wisdom* is applied to in the book of Exodus. Another
way of looking at technology is as the practical application of
scientific knowledge. Technology may be said to be one of
the first implications of the cultural mandate as man became
a tool-maker. There have been many significant technological break-throughs which radically altered the course of
human history. However, until this century the rate at which
technological advances have been made was relatively slow.
The full significance of the invention of the wheel, for
example, would hardly have occurred to those who first used
it. The linking of the use of the lever with that of the wheel
had extraordinary results over a very long period. When
these were together linked with the invention of the steam
engine and, later, the internal combustion engine, the
results came thick and fast. But generally speaking, prior to

---

4. *Letters to Young Churches* (London: Geoffrey Bles, 1947).

the industrial revolution, man had time to adapt to the ramifications of such technological developments. He had more opportunity than we have today to think through the ethical implications of such advances.

But now changes occur so fast that adapting to them is more than man can handle. Now we find that we already have the technology to do many things before we have given enough thought to the ethical implications of doing them. Even though we are more than forty years on from the first harnessing of nuclear energy, the bombing of Hiroshima remains a graphic illustration of the moral dilemmas posed by technology. The debate continues because the implications of Hiroshima are becoming better understood by more and more people. The arms race demonstrates that understanding the issues does not provide the means of controlling the monster that has been created.

The ethical problems created by technology are also clearly seen in the fields of medicine and biology. It is not only Christians who are alarmed by the possible applications of present achievements in in-vitro fertilization, organ transplants and genetic engineering. Many people are saying that research in these areas should be slowed to give us time to think through the issues. Thus, on the one hand it is seen as a race against time to develop new ways of controlling our bodies and our environment in order to achieve some perceived good (babies for the childless, new lease of life for the dying and the abolition of genetic defects such as Down's syndrome). On the other hand there is very great unease about technology for its own sake, about things created for good purposes but with the potential for horrendous harm to society. We are concerned about the depersonalization of the individual and the restriction of certain freedoms. There is little comfort in the secular civil liberties groups, for these often seem to espouse a libertarianism that undermines the Christian concept of well-ordered society. The secular mind that kicks against the idolizing of technology invites the Christian to join in a common cause. But secular groups for nuclear disarmament, alternative life-style, conservation and civil liberties, seldom provide a rationale for action that is really satisfying to the Christian mind.

One of the distinctive problems of modern technology is something that would hardly have presented itself in biblical times. The explosion of knowledge means that more and more people become specialists concentrating on ever narrower fields of knowledge. The specialist is hardly even aware of the vast array of other specializations, let alone of how his field fits in with others. In the light of the biblical view of wisdom and knowledge we see that specialization makes the development of a total world view less probable. The psalmist said:

> Teach us to number our days aright,
> that we may gain a heart of wisdom.   (Psalm 90:12)

For him, this was a matter of life-span as a gift of God. Wisdom, then, reckons on our mortality as something which is bound up with the total order of things as they are now. It is not technology which can teach us the ultimate meaning of our life, for technology was meant to be ruled by what God revealed about this meaning. But specialist technology has all but taken over in matters of birth and death. The ultimate questions have become how to control both the rate and the quality of births, and how long life can and should be prolonged by means of all the technology at our disposal. The individual no longer numbers his days but passes that responsibility over to the technocrats to do it for him.

There must be a multitude of specific considerations for the Christian assessing various aspects of technology. But can we see a broad biblical framework to shape our thinking so that our response is neither mindless conformity nor insecure reaction? I believe we can, and I have no doubt that the biblical concept of wisdom provides the necessary framework. Furthermore, I suspect that the biblical framework may demand some radical re-evaluations of our use of technology. The framework may be relatively simple, but its application to life has the appearance of an ever increasing complexity.

Because science and technology are expressions of the cultural mandate they must be affirmed and welcomed by Christians. Indeed, the Christian view of man and creation

provides the scientist and technologist with a perspective of
their pursuits which not only made them possible, but which
should have prevented them from creating the monster.
When the cultural mandate is accepted on the basis of
revelation, the proper distinctions between God, man
(scientists) and the world can be maintained. But when it
ceases to be seen as mandate, that is, as task authorized by a
superior, it comes to be regarded as the natural extension of
the autonomous man. Removed from its benign relationship
to the order of the universe, it is adopted as the power base
for all kinds of domination. The dominion of man was
intended to reflect the gracious shepherd-rule of God, but it
became corrupted into self-seeking power play. Wisdom
urges us to go on struggling to translate the fear of the Lord
as the beginning of knowledge into the means of living by
faith in the world. Its base in the doctrine of creation, and its
emphasis on the practicalities of life here and now, provide a
check against the wrongful use of an orientation towards the
future life to escape our responsibilities in the present.
Wisdom reminds us that the resurrection life will be reached
by means of our pilgrimage through this life in this world.

If wisdom, which is perfected in the gospel, is to have any
impact in the world, it must be seen as the implication of that
gospel. Far from removing the wisdom literature of the Old
Testament from the concern of Christians, the gospel com-
pletes and interprets it. With the total perspective of Old
and New Testaments we have the basis for understanding
the fear of the Lord and how it brings us to a comprehensive
view of reality. The nature of the unity of all things and the
proper distinction between them are obscured once we have
rejected the ultimate points of reference. The Christian
mind begins with the being of God as Trinity. It is not just
vaguely theistic in some unspecified way. To say, 'I believe
in God' is not good enough unless it is the God of the Bible
we are referring to. The secular mind has rejected this most
significant reference point and has consequently cast a cloud
of ignorance and folly over every area of its knowledge.
Humanism defeats its own goal of the good of man. It
cannot know what is the ultimate good of man since it has
rejected the possibility of the God of the Bible existing. New

gods have taken the place of the true God, and technology has been turned into a particularly tenacious twentieth-century idol. It is a very powerful god since it is the diversion of something that was at the centre of God's purposes for good.

The Israelite was called upon to pursue the good order of the kingdom of God insofar as this was possible in this sinful world. This would have been a meaningless pursuit without the perspective of the future kingdom which God himself would establish by means of the transformation of all things to the perfect order. This was to be the long awaited day of the Lord. According to the New Testament the day of the Lord has come in Jesus Christ, but the old age continues for a time until Christ appears again in glory. Within this overlap of the two ages, between the two comings of Christ, the books of Proverbs, Job and Ecclesiastes are words of God calling us to pursue the order of the kingdom as it applies to this ambiguous age. That order is attained not only through personal conversion and sanctification, but in the communal sanctification of the body of Christ, and through the proclamation of the gospel throughout the world. The gospel judges the disorder that is within us and around us.

The perspective which leads back from Jesus Christ to Old Testament wisdom and then to the creation, reminds us that the transformation to order that we so earnestly desire in ourselves will not happen without the transformation of the whole person, body, mind and spirit, and of the universe around us. It is impossible for us to imagine what the complete absence of disorder will mean in the new earth. The anticipation of that experience is one of the joys of holding to the certainty of our resurrection on the last day. But it is never solely anticipation, for the process of transforming us to that order has already begun from the moment Christ takes hold of us through his gospel. The wisdom literature of the Old Testament plays a vital part in structuring for us the inevitable effect of the gospel in our lives as we are transformed by the renewing of our minds (Romans 12:2).

In an age when technology and the race to possess it have replaced the ancient tribal rivalries, the wise men of Israel remind us that the word *wisdom* was, at least for a while, a synonym for technology as it then existed. These sages are worthy companions as we press on towards the cosmic regeneration. In unexpected ways they teach us trust and the fear of the Lord. In doing so, they compel us to the source of true wisdom in the person and work of Christ. He who is the way, the truth and the life, remains the beginning and the goal of every man's search for order and meaning in the universe. The men of Israel may surprise and even offend us with their earthiness and home-spun wisdom. At times we may find it difficult to recognize God's voice speaking to us through them. But God's highest wisdom was himself to become one with them and us as the God-man. Thus he made the world our classroom. Whether we consider the ways of Solomon's ant, ponder Job's leviathan, or marvel with Qohelet at life's deepest mysteries, Christ alone will transform all the distortions and ambiguities of our myopic view. He is our Wisdom, and thus turns the words of the ancient Hebrew wise men into the urgent proclamation of the gospel which summons us to trust him for everything that is in life;

> Blessed is the man who listens to me,
> watching daily at my doors,
> waiting at my doorway.
> For whoever finds me finds life
> and receives favour from the Lord.

(Proverbs 8:34–35)

Questions for study

1. Why must all Old Testament texts be understood in the light of the gospel?
2. On what biblical evidence may we build our understanding of what Paul referred to as the gift of wisdom in 1 Corinthians 12:8?
3. How does the biblical concept of wisdom help us understand the nature of guidance and decision-making?
4. How does biblical wisdom help us address the gospel to this technological age?

Indexes

Index of subjects and names

Index of references to Scripture and Apocrypha

OLD TESTAMENT

APOCRYPHA

NEW TESTAMENT

Gospel and Kingdom
A Christian Interpretation of the Old Testament

Graeme Goldsworthy

In an engaging and straightforward style, the author explains the nature and contents of the Old Testament as seen within the Bible as a whole and sets out clear principles for interpreting it accurately for today.

ISBN 0-85364-608-2

PATERNOSTER
PRESS
CARLISLE, UNITED KINGDOM

The Gospel in Revelation
Gospel and Apocalypse

Graeme Goldsworthy

In his characteristically pithy and lucid style, Goldsworthy offers here a fresh understanding of the purpose and contemporary relevance of Revelation, arguing that the gospel is the key to unlocking its meaning. This exemplary study is further informed by the author's knowledge of Old Testament literary idiom and structure.

ISBN 0-85364-630-9

PATERNOSTER
PRESS
CARLISLE, UNITED KINGDOM

Jonah
An Exposition

R.T. Kendall

It was with this series of sermons that Kendall inaugurated his ministry at Westminster Chapel. They are presented here almost as they were delivered in order to retain their freshness and authenticity. As a result, the message that heralded a new beginning for one congregation twenty years ago can speak powerfully to many others today.

ISBN 0-85364-653-8

PATERNOSTER PRESS

CARLISLE, UNITED KINGDOM

Believing God
Studies on Faith in Hebrews 11

R.T. Kendall

It was Martyn Lloyd-Jones who lent Kendall the expression 'Believing God' as a definition of faith. And focusing on the mighty stalwarts of faith catalogued in Hebrews 11, Kendall is at pains to remind us that the writer of the Epistle was more concerned about the nature of faith itself than about these people of faith.

ISBN 0-85364-652-x

PATERNOSTER PRESS

CARLISLE, UNITED KINGDOM

EUROPEAN
THEOLOGICAL MEDIA

For a book service that offers you up-to-date
information on new publications and discounts of
up to 50% on a wide range of academic titles, ask
for the free Nota Bene quarterly catalogue from:

European Theological Media, PO Box 777,
Carlisle, Cumbria CA3 0QS, UK.